WHAT TO DO

When You Don't Want to Go to Church

WHAT TO DO

When You Don't Want to Go to Church

PeggySue Wells & Pat Palau
Foreword by Luis Palau

Advancing the Ministries of the Gospel
AMG *Publishers*

God's Word to you is our highest calling.

What to Do When You Don't Want to Go to Church

Published by AMG Publishers
6815 Shallowford Rd.
Chattanooga, TN 37421

ISBN 0-89957-353-3

First printing—February 2004

Cover designed by Market Street Design, Chattanooga, Tennessee
Interior design and typesetting by Reider Publishing Services,
    West Hollywood, California
Edited and Proofread by David and Renée Sanford (Sanford
    Communications, Inc., Portland, Oregon), Dan Penwell,
    Warren Baker, and Jody El-Assadi

Printed in the United States of America
10 09 08 07 06 05 04 –D– 8 7 6 5 4 3 2 1

To Pastor Albert and Roberta Wollen,
who taught me to love
and serve the Church and its Savior,
faithfully modeling Jesus to me
for more than thirty years.

—*Patricia*

To AmyRose, Leilani, Holly, Josiah,
Estee, Hannah, and Lilyanna,
and to The Chapel, my church family.

—*PeggySue*

"Let us hold unswervingly to the hope we profess, for he who promised is faithful. And let us consider how we may spur one another on toward love and good deeds. Let us not give up meeting together, as some are in the habit of doing, but let us encourage one another—and all the more as you see the Day approaching."

—HEBREWS 10:23–25

Contents

Foreword

My wife Pat and I are active members of a church near our home in Portland, Oregon. Although we travel a good part of every year to minister in evangelism throughout the United States and overseas, we're not excused from taking part in our church and remaining in subjection to the elders. We find it's important to consult with them on major decisions involving our family and sometimes even our evangelistic team.

My advice to every Christian is the same: Attend church regularly. Follow the prescribed procedures to become a member of your local church. Inform the church leaders that your desire is to become an active member and work positively and productively under their leadership.

Even though our churches are not without fault, don't allow yourself to develop a critical spirit. "I appeal to you, brothers, in the name of our Lord Jesus Christ, that all of you agree with one another so that there may be no divisions among you and that you may be perfectly united in mind and thought" (1 Corinthians 1:10). Your church is your "family" in Christ. Defend it! When others grumble, remind them to take the matter to the elders, not to the rest of the Christians in your church. After all, some church members are not mature and many others are not gifted to help resolve tough issues.

Sometimes, because of other commitments, I face pressures to pull back and limit my participation in the local church. But I'm convinced from Scripture and experience that as I continue planting my roots deeply into the local church, I will be the winner in the long run.

This practical, sometimes humorous, biblically-based book will help tens of thousands of Christians settle a vital issue in their daily lives. I like the quotes, interviews, and down-to-earth comments. It makes this book sparkle and motivates you to keep reading.

I've observed the energetic and hard work PeggySue and Pat have put into this book. I believe pastors will appreciate the encouragement it gives to their work. It honors God in his own Church. The book effectively puts before you the great advantages, divine reasons, and personal profit of a consistent church commitment and active service.

I challenge you to reevaluate the importance of the local church in your own life. Now is a good time to begin anew!

—*Luis Palau*

Acknowledgments

Heartfelt thanks to:

Our many gracious contributors. You are the heart-beat of this book.

Mary Ann Froehlich who set this project in motion and cheered its progress to completion.

David and Renée Sanford who understood the intent of this book, and thus, did a superb job of editing.

Dan Penwell and the professionals at AMG Publishers, who believe that church matters because of Jesus Christ.

Introduction

> *It is not you that sings, it is the church that is singing, and you, as a member...may share in its song. Thus all singing [together] that is right must serve to widen our spiritual horizon, make us see our little company as a member of the great Christian Church on earth, and help us willingly and gladly to join our singing, be it feeble or good, to the song of the Church.*
>
> —DIETRICH BONHOEFFER, *Life Together*

We don't want to admit it, but we have all experienced it. Sunday morning arrives and the last place we want to go is church.

It starts out legitimately enough. You're unusually tired for good reasons. You've been helping a friend. Church hasn't been inspiring lately. The preacher is new and you're finding it hard to get used to the innovations he's brought with him. Sunday is a day of rest and it would be good to just rest up. After all, this next week already is looking stressful.

The problem is that this mental conversation happened six months ago and the excuses kept piling up until you've lost the churchgoing habit. Sometimes you feel guilty, but plenty of people around you are doing likewise. In fact, for the past year you've been the only one on your block who bothered to go to church on Sunday morning. You didn't intend to drop out of church, but you have. What difference does it make, anyhow?

Perhaps you've been fighting with your spouse and kids and seeing all those happy families sitting in the pews multiplies your despair. Maybe it's not just that you're having a bad weekend. Instead, painful childhood associations make church feel like an unsafe place for you. Church feels more about activities than relationships. A conflict makes you uncomfortable when you see a particular someone at church. Aware that you are not part of the "in" clique at church, perhaps you feel betrayed that the community of believers has been reduced to a social club.

And the list goes on. Alone, the reasons seem immature, childish, or unworthy. But they begin to pile up, and in honest moments we say, "I don't want to go anymore."

Sometimes you feel the farthest from God when sitting in a church service. Perhaps you never feel lonelier than when you attend church. Why? Through the seasons of our lives the reasons can be endless for why we dread going to church.

Whether your issues with the church began with a big bang or as a slow leak, is church attendance really that important?

Pat and PeggySue each came to faith on a different path. While PeggySue's family attended church in her early years, her childhood home consisted of chaos, abuse, neglect, and abandonment. Because divorce was considered the unforgivable sin, the church shunned and rejected PeggySue when her parents divorced. Years later, married and expecting their first child, PeggySue and her husband returned to church in hopes of raising their children in an authentic relationship with Jesus Christ. With her newborn in her arms, PeggySue rededicated her life to the Lord.

Pat's story reads much differently. On the day of Pat's birth, her grandparents gave Pat's parents a copy of D.L. Moody's *Wondrous Love*. On the flyleaf, Grandma inscribed:

To Elsie and Willard on Patricia's birth.
May her sweet little life be dedicated to Him
whose wondrous love never fails.
John 3:16
from, Mother
June 24, 1937

Though Pat's grandparents had recently placed their faith in Jesus Christ, Pat's parents were not Christians and avoided all conversations on religious subjects. But that did not stop Pat's grandparents from communicating, by word and example, the Good News of Jesus Christ. Within several years both of Pat's parents trusted the Lord Jesus as their Savior, and at age eight, Pat did too.

Pat's grandmother did not know Pat would marry an evangelist and that, together, Pat and Luis Palau would invest their lives preaching the Gospel world-wide. But God rewarded that grandmother's desire to impart a godly inheritance to her family.

Today Pat and Luis have four sons, four daughters-in-law, and nine grandchildren (at last count!). The Palaus make their home in Portland, Oregon, near the international headquarters of the Luis Palau Evangelistic Association. Pat attends the same church her grandparents helped found and where her parents stabilized their faith.

For this book, we asked contributors to share what encourages them to attend church and what discourages them. We asked adults what their parents and church did to encourage their faith and what actions discouraged their faith as children. We asked prodigals what brought them back to their faith. We asked those who did not grow up in Christian homes who mirrored Jesus Christ to them. We discovered what spiritual traditions help keep believers anchored. Finally, we explored the deep woundedness and conflict that occurs within the church, and the great hope that comes in healing and reconciliation, acceptance of our own fallen human nature, and God's grace.

> *When I first became a Christian . . . I thought that I could do it on my own, by retiring to my rooms and reading theology, and I wouldn't go to the churches. . . . I disliked very much their hymns, which I considered to be fifth-rate poems set to sixth-rate music. But as I went on I saw the great merit of it. I came up against different people of quite different outlooks and different education, and then gradually my conceit just began peeling off. I realized that the hymns [were] being sung with devotion and benefit by an old saint in elastic-side boots in the opposite pew, and then you realize that you aren't fit to clean those boots. It gets you out of your solitary conceit.*
>
> —C. S. LEWIS, *God in the Dock*

The Church with a Capital "C"

The Christian life is not just our own private affair. If we have been born again into God's family, not only has he become our Father but every other Christian believer in the world, whatever his nation or denomination, has become our brother or sister in Christ. [B]ut it is no good supposing that member-ship in the universal Church of Christ is enough; we must belong to some local branch of it. . . . Every Christian's place is in a local church . . . sharing in its worship, its fellowship, and its witness.

— JOHN STOTT,
Basic Christianity

I became interested in the subject of the Church, and going to church, because I had friends who were between churches. They called themselves "nonchurch-going" Christians. These friends said they had better things to do on Sunday morning than attend church.

Indeed, with so many demands on our already limited time, why should we spend a perfectly good Sunday morning going to church?

It's vital to remember that we use the word *church* in two ways—the Church with the capital "C" and the church with the small "c." All believers in Jesus Christ, all born-again Christians, are members of the worldwide Church with the capital C. The local congregation is the church with the lower case ĉ.

The church with the little c has left us with negative thoughts about church. Most feelings of alienation and disconnection appear when we are trying to find a local church home to settle into. The key words that define church are *connecting* and *belonging*. We long to belong and feel connected.

Jesus personally invited people to come into the Church through a relationship with him. Our assurance that we are related to Jesus Christ and he loves us, that God is our Father and we are his children, is what binds us together as the body of Christ, "for we are members of his body" (Ephesians 5:30). Belonging to *that* family, with a capital C, makes us feel comfortable to be part of any church family that really is part of that great body of Christ.

While attending churches in faraway places like Turkey or India, I have been overcome emotionally because of the connectedness I felt with believers whose language I couldn't even speak. They didn't look like me and didn't worship like me, but we were united as part of the big Church with the capital C, the body of Christ.

In some places and under some circumstances, however, people can be stinky. Leadership can be less than godly. In unhealthy situations, unbiblical forms of dictatorial leadership can exist. In toxic situations, people can lose their ability to reason, to walk before God as individuals, and to exercise their own freedom in Jesus Christ. But that should be the exception rather than the rule.

The disconnect we feel when making the decision to unite with a little c chapter of the body of Christ does not come because of details like the way we sing, the way we sit, or the pitch of the pastor's voice. It goes back to how connected we are with Jesus Christ himself.

The church with the small c consists of a percentage of people who have no assurance of a clinching experience in which they came to Jesus for rest and forgiveness. Each of us must come to Jesus, who said, "I am the way and the truth and the life. No one comes to the Father except through me" (John 14:6). We are desperately needy sinners—desperately in need of a Savior! Until we truly connect to the Savior, our connection to a local group of Christians will not be complete.

"Come to Me"

People are stressed, alienated, isolated, and uncomfortable most of the time. Jesus says, "Come to me, all you who are weary and burdened, and I will give you rest. Take my yoke upon you and learn from me, for I am gentle and humble in heart, and you will find rest for your souls. For my yoke is easy and my burden is light" (Matthew 11:28–30).

Jesus described us as "weary and burdened." Our international ministry, the Luis Palau Evangelistic Association, once conducted a survey in the North Shore area of Chicago where people live very well. Most of us would offer to change places with them any day. Yet the young middle-class women said they felt exhausted, confused about too many choices, and burned out. Not weary and burdened like people in other parts of the world who scrape to get enough food to eat, for sure. But they are weary and burdened with their busy lives, struggling to balance the need for solitude, personal fulfillment, and dealing with the overwhelming needs of others.

Exhausted people are characterized by ceaseless activity that doesn't get us any closer to the Kingdom, any closer to knowing Jesus better, or even any closer to getting our house clean. The rest of the world laughs at us restless Americans because we are constantly changing and never settled. What is here today is gone tomorrow, and the church reflects those trends.

Sometimes we are weary and burdened by unrealistic standards, fearful of being considered failures. Listen to this paraphrase of: "Are you tired? Worn out? Burned out on religion? Come to me. Get away with me and you will recover your life. I will show you how to take real rest. Walk with me and work with me—watch how I do it. Learn the unforced rhythms of grace. I won't lay anything heavy or ill fitting on you. Keep company with me and you'll learn to live freely and lightly" (Matthew 11:28–30, *THE MESSAGE*).

"I Will Give You Rest"

Jesus Christ does not call us to attend another class or program, but to come directly to him. We have a choice between rest and stress. We all know the meaning of stress. Come to Jesus the Counselor for understanding, to Jesus the Mighty God for comfort, to Jesus the Prince of Peace for rest because he is the only one who truly meets all our needs.

I have never found anyone eager to sit around and listen to me whine about the uniqueness of my life. Have you ever shared your intense struggle only to have your listener respond, "That's nothing," and proceed to best your story with one of his or her own? Instead, the apostle Paul tells us, "each one should carry his own load" (Galatians 6:5).

People can only empathize so far. Jesus said come daily to *him* for the issues that steal our rest—guilt, sin, frustration—and for all the things that define who we really are. If we find two or three friends in a lifetime that catch segments of who we are, we thank the Lord for them. Accepting people for what they bring into our life, we cannot expect them to understand us perfectly. The only one who understands perfectly is the one who made you and me. That goes for churches, too. It is fruitless to expect from fellow human beings the love, acceptance, and forgiveness that only God can give.

Jesus said, "I will give you rest," and he meant eternal rest. Nothing else matters except this: that our relationship with him is settled. When you have that kind of rest, you will move into the church with the little c and feel comfortable. If you are not settled in heaven as a home, you will not feel settled in any earthly relationships.

The rest Jesus promises is a sense of being refreshed and alive and quieted on the inside. Ultimate rest is forgiveness for my soul. It is settled once at the foot of the cross where Jesus paid for my sins and shortcomings and is reaffirmed on a daily basis. Eternal rest means knowing that heaven is my home so, whatever happens to me here, I'm okay and I can live with it. Nothing can separate me from God's love.

"My Yoke Is Easy and My Burden Is Light"

The yoke is an opportunity to willingly join Jesus in a personal tutor/learner relationship. If something is bothering me when I'm yoked up close, I only have to turn my head to see Jesus. Then I remember that Jesus is where I go for guidance.

As God's children, we are free to ask why. God is always willing to offer guidance. Circumstances are not always easy; relationships are sometimes complex. Your status and acceptance by God is about you; it is not about all the people around you. You do not have to compete with the world. God forgives you, loves you, accepts you, and changes you so that you can relax while yoked to him. When Jesus is in you, the Holy Spirit is your teacher. It works!

We often design our own yokes of leadership, volunteering, and other self-inflicted punishments. Neither easy nor light, self-designed yokes are crushing. Anytime our focus is not on Jesus, but on those around us, we're headed straight to burnout.

Instead, we need to carefully manage our time and stay within the areas where God has gifted us. God created you and me, he planned our life, and he knows what comes naturally to each of us. We keep first things first by carving out pockets of time for reflection, to think things through, to wait and be still, and to test what we hear through Scripture. When we are yoked to Jesus Christ, the burden is his—he carries it for us.

"And you shall find rest for your souls" refers to our daily experience of coming constantly to commit, confess, and restore our communion with him. Rest for our souls brings eternal life because of the perfect work of Jesus Christ on the cross. Rest for our souls frees our conscience from guilt. We come once for cleansing from sin and daily for renewed relationship.

Jesus' description of himself as "gentle and humble in heart" doesn't apply to some of the churches we've been in. That's why we always look to him. Anytime we fix our eyes on people, we will be disappointed.

The leadership of Jesus Christ is not characterized by rules, harshness, or demands without sense or reason. There is no "because I said so, that's why!" Yoked to Jesus, we can hear his quiet voice guiding us. Dr. Haddon Robinson from Gordon-Conwell Seminary once said, "I learned that God loved me just as I was . . .

but too much to leave me that way." Whatever God asks us to do, he equips us to do.

So Why Belong to a Local Church?

We join a church because we all have the same heavenly Father, we are a family, and a family treats each other well. In my own household, I don't suddenly ask two of my immediate family members to continue living with me and tell the rest to go live somewhere else. It might have crossed my mind, but I don't do that because they are born into *my family*. In the same way, we are all born into God's family and, one way or the other, we need to learn to live together.

The reasoning that says "I am the Church because I belong to Jesus Christ, so I don't need to attend a local church" bothers me. "Wherever I am, that's church" sounds cool, but it's wrong. True, I'm away from my home church often, but if I'm at home, I'm there. God doesn't keep score, but Scripture commands us to regularly get together in some form or another for our own sake and for the sake of other believers (see Hebrews 10:25).

It's amazing how devious our minds are. I can think of many reasons not to attend church: "I've been around a lot of Christians this week, I've heard a lot of messages, I've sung a lot of songs, so what's the big deal? Why do I need to go to church on this particular day?"

Still, I need to go to church because everybody else is going and I belong to and am connected to them. Regular worship in the company of other believers sets my spiritual compass and takes my spiritual temperature.

All week you and I see things materialistically, humanly, as if "that's all there is." Worship pulls back the curtains so I can see the real picture about God, the universe, and my place in it. Attending church is the best way for me to grow and develop my spiritual gifts. I cannot grow in isolation. I need to hear voices other than my own.

When we experience troubles, other Christians will help—if they know us. If you are ever going to get sick or die, you better be in a church that knows you because otherwise nobody is going to comfort you or plan your funeral. I have a friend who likes a television preacher who has more charm and zip than the pastor of the church that I attend, but that television personality is not going to conduct her funeral!

When we belong to the body of Christ, we get into a church family and live with it through thick and thin, year after year after year. Being thirty or forty years in the same place teaches me about families and how God is making them better and better. When someone asks me, "What about the Smiths and the Lees?" I say, "I've known them since their parents were kids and you can't believe how much better they function now than they used to a long time ago."

Seeing the slow, imperceptible growth in families and in myself is the wonderful side of being in a church for a long time. I know people better. The church with the little c is a laboratory where we test things out, we learn to do things, and people give us a chance. All kinds of opportunities arise where I can learn and serve in a local church that wants me to grow.

I can sincerely say good things about most of the churches I know anything about. True, all churches have ups and downs. None of us do well with change and change is a frequent catalyst for discomfort in the church. But I can weather it if what holds me together with others is the absolute assurance that I am God's child.

When I was in my thirties I remember telling an elder in our church that I wasn't happy. I didn't feel comfortable. I wasn't appreciated. There were a lot of changes going on. He patted my shoulder and said I would feel better eventually. He did not revamp everything the way I wanted it. How glad I am that I stayed! The issues are long since forgotten.

Connecting and Belonging

I know what it's like not to feel quite at home. I don't like it when I enter a group and there are asides, humor, or nicknames and everyone laughs except me because I don't have any idea what they are talking about. Often people make announcements about upcoming events using the initials of the group, and I don't know if it is a program that pertains to me or not.

A healthy church is considerate of those working to develop a sense of belonging. For my part, the better I understand who I am as a member of the body of Christ—the big C Church—the better I can laugh off the awkward moments and know that one of these days I will feel comfortable. My feelings are not as important as simply making a prayerful commitment that this is where I'm going to settle and grow. I grow as I push myself to go where I don't want to go and do things that are not in my comfort zone. Slowly I begin to feel at home.

There is a difference between *being* at home and *feeling* at home. The church *is* your home even though it may not feel like it for a long time. One day you will realize you have settled in and feel comfortable.

What Is a Great Church?

People in the church are not perfect. Jesus said, "It is not the healthy who need a doctor, but the sick" (Matthew 9:12). When you bounce from church to church, everybody appears godly and perfect. You aren't there long enough to know there is another side. You don't know reality. The church is an asset, a tool, a community, a fellowship, and a place where we ought to be.

A great church majors in helping people know Jesus Christ and grow in their relationship with him. Unfortunately, we humans don't balance things well. A church that is good at evangelism often isn't good at growing the baby Christians they have birthed. I also know a church where they have an evangelistic service every Sunday night, but there hasn't been a non-Christian there in probably thirty years. They preach the same message every Sunday night, but only because it's a habit and it's beyond questioning.

A great church values God's Word, consistently puts out the Scripture for us to look at, allows us to ask questions, and lets the Word speak for itself. Together we bring glory to God through worship, fellowship, community, evangelism, prayer, Bible study, Christian education, and outreach. Through these activities, we "spur one another on toward love and good deeds" (Hebrews 10:24).

A great church has leaders who demonstrate the gifts of the Holy Spirit for leading the community of believers. But the Bible does not place a higher value on those who lead than on those who are led. All of us lead in some venue somewhere. We are both learners and leaders at the same time. We do both simultaneously. The church is a grouping of people who are in the process—with the leading of the Holy Spirit—of equipping each one to be ministers of the Gospel of Jesus Christ. The goal of the church is "to prepare God's people for works of service, so that the body of Christ may be built up" (Ephesians 4:12).

Church Matters!

- It matters to God that I go to church. Jesus went to synagogue on the Sabbath and if ever a person had good reason not to go, he did! He went to teach and be a blessing, and to set an example of what you and I should do.
- I go to church to celebrate Jesus. I explained this one Sunday morning to the whiners in the back of my station wagon. I go because it is the day of remembrance of his resurrection, and I don't think one part of one day a week is too much to ask.
- I go to church because it matters to me. It matters to my family, who watch me. It does not mean that every time I come out of church I say, "Wow! That was fabulous." But I'm always glad I went. It's where I belong, and more times than not I have been blessed in many ways.
- It matters to me that I go to church because there I am surrounded by others who share the same spiritual journey. We help each other. I prayed that my children would grow up and marry fellow believers in Jesus Christ. I figured

the best place for them to network with other young people who would be their friends was in a church where I had roots and they were happy.

- It matters to the community that I go to church. People look to the church as a place where they can go and receive comfort and encouragement. All kinds of people come to church when there is a tragedy. It matters to the community that the church is there.

- It matters to my health that I rest on Sunday. We have forgotten that. When I was growing up, people didn't do anything that looked like work on Sundays. Businesses were closed. I try to resist things that steal my day of rest, but I'm drowning in a culture that wants to do everything all the time. I long for a simpler life, but today there are so many things I can do on Sundays. God designed a day of rest to relax, read, enjoy music, and converse with God and others. Taking an hour to sit still, to sing, and hear God's Word is a great start.

- I go to church to focus on stillness. To grow spiritually, you and I can practice spiritual disciplines such as Bible reading, Scripture memorization, fasting, and prayer. But we are not monks. We do not live where the phone doesn't ring, and these disciplines are not practiced as much as they might be. Uniting with others challenges me to persevere in healthy spiritual disciplines.

- I come to worship the Father, Son, and Holy Spirit. No church program is so awkward that it thwarts my experience of worshiping the Lord. Some people complain they don't get anything out of church or it doesn't meet their needs. In *The Purpose-Driven Life*, Rick Warren reminds us: "If you have ever said, 'I didn't get anything out of worship today,' you worshiped for the wrong reason. Worship isn't for you. It's for God." I can worship God anywhere—even in church. Going to church and exercising my spiritual gifts in the midst of other Christians is a normal part of the spiritual service of worship God expects of me (see Romans 12:1–13).

- I go to church to bless others. I don't have something special to say to everyone, but some people are blessed if I simply know their name, pat them on the shoulder, and recognize that they are there. Other times, our weekly gathering in Christ's name sparks remarkable, even life-changing, conversations.

- I come to be obedient to God. Hebrews 10:24, 25 exhorts: "Let's see how inventive we can be in encouraging love and helping out, not avoiding worshiping together as some do, but spurring each other on especially as we see the big day approaching" (*THE MESSAGE*).

Learning to Live in the Family

People claim they've gotten out of the habit of going to church. They say they don't miss it, they don't enjoy church, or they had bad experiences as a child. The saddest stories I've heard about the church with the little c reveal a terrible lack of grace. But we are grown-ups, we are big enough to acknowledge gracelessness exists, and we can ask God to help us to be full of grace in our own attitudes toward others.

If you belong to Jesus Christ, you belong to his body wherever it might be. The church with the little c is yours! We all have similar needs to connect and belong. My children don't leave my family because they say I don't meet their needs. They might say it, but it doesn't change anything. I worship where I worship not because it's perfect, but because it's where God wants us as a family. Find ways to help others grow. Join a small group where you can know and be known and establish roots in the church. There is no substitute for the church with the little c.

A friend told me she changed churches yet another time. I said, "Fine, but don't do it again." We need to find one church and settle in. A weekly appointment together with God and his children is therapeutic.

In John 14:2, Jesus said, "I am going there to prepare a place for you." Someday he'll come back and take us to heaven. Heaven is your real home. Heaven is not now. There will always be something wrong with everything we do, with every relationship. This life is not *it*; this is only the training ground for eternal *life*. The local assembly of believers is a preparation for the heaven that will be ours one day. Any momentary sense of discomfort simply reminds us that we are not home yet. Until Jesus Christ returns, the church is where God has put each of us to bless and be blessed.

The Church with the capital C makes us a Christian, a member of Christ's body. The church with the small "c" is our family, our haven, our home on earth. It is where we truly belong.

You will notice we say "brother and sister" 'round
     here
It's because we're a family and these folks are so
     near;
When one has a heartache we all share the tears,
And rejoice in each victory in this family so dear.
From the door of an orphanage to the house of
     the King

No longer an outcast, a new song I sing,
From rags unto riches, from the weak to the strong,
I'm not worthy to be here, but praise God, I belong!
I'm so glad I'm a part of the family of God,
I've been washed in the fountain, cleansed by his
blood!
Joint heirs with Jesus as we travel this sod,
For I'm part of the family of God.

> — *The Family of God*
> Words by William J. and Gloria Gaither.
> Music by William J. Gaither.
> Copyright © 1970 William J. Gaither, Inc.
> All rights controlled by Gaither Copyright
> Management.
> Used by permission. (Inspired by an
> accident that left a fellow church
> member badly burned. The congregation
> prayed around the clock until it was
> announced on Easter Sunday that the
> man would live.)

SECTION I

The Church
as Encourager

The Church Triumphant

The strength of a church isn't seen in the width of their sanctuary. It's seen in the width of their arms that circle you.

—CHURCH BULLETIN

What is the bottom line for being part of Christ's church and becoming a mature believer? The answers are the same for all Christians, of all times, in all places. Everything we Americans do is almost instantly outdated, but one of the strongest arguments for the truth of the Gospel is that it fits everyone everywhere. It always has and always will.

I saw a beautiful example of the simplicity of the church on a trip to South Asia. It was my third visit to a biweekly Bible study on a rooftop in a city of ten million, and I worshiped with sixty-two other women of all ages, many of them elderly. A missionary, Colleen Redit, has led this Bible study for three decades.

They took roll and the women answered with a memorized verse. Married to rigidly religious men who forbid contact with Christianity, most did not keep the Scriptures in their homes, yet these women had an amazing knowledge of the Bible, able to recite long chapters. Anytime I slowed down in my presentation, they filled in the gaps. Fifteen of these women had been involved since the ministry's early days, and an equal number had gone on to heaven.

At the conclusion of the Bible study, the women covered their heads with their beautiful saris and folded their hands in an attitude of worship. An older woman began to pray. For ten minutes she proclaimed adoration and praise for God, exalting his name and character.

What is the secret of their perseverance? These women take Jesus at his word. They thrive spiritually on a basic diet of fundamental truths and constant communion. "Whom have I in heaven but you? And earth has nothing I desire besides you" (Psalm 73:25). What would I be like if I lived in that atmosphere of trust in God's character and goodness? This is the church of Jesus Christ, adapting to persecution, worshipping secretly on a rooftop at sunset on a Monday.

Awarding-winning author Philip Yancey wrote: "In my own travels overseas, I have noticed a striking difference in the wording of prayers. When difficulties come, Christians in affluent countries tend to pray, 'Lord, take this trial away from us!' I have heard persecuted Christians and some that live in very poor countries pray instead, 'Lord, give us the strength to bear this trial.'"

We all have nasty disappointments and tragedies, but where is God and what is he like? That is the universal question.

> *There are two things we cannot do alone.*
> *One is to be married and the other is to be a*
>   *Christian.*

—PAUL TOURNIER

What Others Say about the Church

My home church has been an important part of my life since I became a Christian at age forty-one. Being part of a church family, I always received more than I gave. After fifteen years, I moved out of state and was looking for a church in my new town when I got the phone call every parent dreads. My adult daughter had died. I had to get to her and the rest of my family, but I was in no shape emotionally to make the long and difficult drive over mountain passes. This is where being connected to a local church meant so much. Barely able to think, I prayed for God to bring to mind someone I could call to help. Then I thought of a darling, elderly couple from a church I had visited. I called them and they found just the right person who drove me to that faraway hospital where my daughter was. I was a relative newcomer, but that church—now my home church—embraced me with their love and care. They exemplified the body of Christ reaching out and loving me.

I grew up in a large, chaotic family. The same year I graduated from high school, my alcoholic parents divorced, and I discovered I was pregnant. Four babies later, I was divorced, lonely, and felt like a failure. Desperate for a solid foundation in my life, I went to church. That body of Christians warmly welcomed my children and me without judgment. Twenty years later, I am still a member of that same congregation where I have a vibrant ministry to others who are hurting because of a difficult marriage. The acceptance of the church changed my life.

In a letter to the editor of the newspaper, a churchgoer complained that it made no sense to attend church. "I've gone for thirty years now," he wrote, "and in that time I have heard something like three thousand sermons. But for the life of me I can't remember a single one of them. I'm wasting my time and pastors are wasting their time giving sermons." This sparked a controversy in the "Letters to the Editor" column until someone wrote this clincher: "I've been married for thirty years now. In that time my wife has cooked some thirty-two thousand meals. But for the life of me, I cannot recall what the menu was for a single one of those meals. But I do know this: they all nourished me and gave me the strength I needed to do my work. If my wife had not given me those meals, I would be dead today."

As a new believer I began attending a local church. One young mother frequently prayed aloud during the corporate worship time. I could sense that her fervent, heartfelt prayers exalting and praising God were an embarrassment to many people in the church, but I longed to know the God she knew and pray like she did. That woman's prayers ignitcd a firc in me to get to know the Word of God and study the attributes of God.

Our pastor encouraged my faith to grow in leaps and bounds by having the most open pulpit possible. Every missionary who came through our area was invited to speak to the congregation. Parachurch organizations were given opportunity to tell about their work within the community, and anyone who had a testimony was asked to share it with the church. Our pastor frequently brought prayer requests from neighboring churches to our congregation and occasionally traded pulpits with other local pastors on Sunday mornings, benefiting both congregations.

Twice a year, our church gathered with all the other community churches to form one giant entry in the city parade. Atop a decorated flatbed truck, a combined worship team led spirited worship music while the congregations marched behind singing and carrying banners representing area churches and parachurch organizations. Prize money from the parade entry was divided to support the community's parachurch ministries.

Because he was not jealous of his pulpit, our pastor exposed our congregation to a vast number of contemporary saints and broadened my view of the Christian family far beyond the four walls of that church building.

I grew up in a religious home, but not a Christian home. After I married, I began attending my husband's church. Though I had never seen the altar used at my childhood church, people at my new church used the altar frequently. As they talked about a personal relationship with Jesus Christ, I saw something different in these people. I attended a Sunday school class for young married people where the teacher cared about each of us young women. An older married woman, she was genuinely concerned about our marriages and shared the excitement of her own vivacious marriage. Her example and teaching have been the foundation for my own twenty-five-year marriage.

Occasionally I am asked to speak at churches. As I prepared for a weekend at a church I had never been to and with people I had never met, a note arrived in the mail. It read, "I am praying for you as the Lord leads you to share with us. I am really looking forward to meeting you." What encouragement to know someone I had not even met was praying for me.

To allow young mothers, exhausted from caring for small children all week, to be rested and refreshed both physically and spiritually, our church hired an experienced grandma to tend the nursery. The babies and toddlers quickly warmed to her because the same smiling face cared for them every week. Since this loving woman attended the Seventh Day Adventist church on Saturday, we did not interfere with her own worship time. Mature Christian men, our church's elders and deacons, mentored our youngsters by teaching the children's and teens' classes. The church valued our children and took pains to surround them with only the best influences.

My son's departure from the faith coincided with my own life-threatening bout with cancer. My life was in crisis physically and spiritually. For both concerns I turned to the writings of Amy Carmichael. She is a source I still turn to even though she has been dead for half a century. As a missionary in India, Amy Carmichael cared for thousands of abandoned and abused children for decades. Single, yet mothering beyond what I could hold to my heart, she reached out with the love of the Father to those who disappointed her and she pleaded their case. Her ability to put into words the deep groaning of the suffering soul brought great comfort. Like Paul who said, "Whatever you have learned or received or heard from me, or seen in me—put it into practice" (Philippians 4:9), she left spiritual footsteps for me to follow. The examples of believers who have gone before me are an inspiration for my own spiritual journey.

The churches in my town joined together to renovate a home and convert it into a Bible-based ministry for drug-addicted mothers. Their combined sponsorship provided an opportunity for many women to get off drugs and come to know Jesus Christ as their Lord and Savior. The ministry project was an avenue for Christians from many denominations to minister together to our shared community.

When my husband abandoned our family, the church subsidized my children's school tuition and church camps, provided counseling for us, and occasionally sent a team over to make minor household repairs. The church eagerly stepped into the role of extended family, and my children and I learned to run to Jesus during the challenges of life.

Our church leadership regularly shared the ministry's vision and purpose with the congregation. Knowing where we were going, what the big picture was, kept our eyes on growing spiritually and reaching out to our community. United on the larger goal greater than ourselves, the church rarely got sidetracked on minor issues.

Rough around the edges and unmarried, I began attending church. When I announced I was pregnant, the older women in the congregation cheered. They rallied around me with food, clothes, and furniture. They slipped much needed money to me. Those women wrapped my baby and me in the assurance that we were part of this family. When my son was born, the women passed him from one set of waiting arms to another. Years later my son and I still attend that church and those loving women hug us each week. They love us, and we love them. We are family.

Recognizing the growing trend of grandparents rearing their grandchildren, our church established a ministry to encourage grandparents who found themselves parenting again. This ministry provided activities for the children and opportunities for the grandparents to have a respite. In addition to providing counseling services, the church paired each child with a mentor in the career field the child wanted to pursue. When needed, the church paid for the children to attend college.

Our church viewed itself as the pep rally before the big game of life that began each Monday. The music and sermon was geared to inspire, equip, and send us out to carry the Gospel to the world until we met again the next week.

A school friend invited me to church when I was seven years old. After I married, someone invited me to Bible Study Fellowship where I accepted Jesus Christ as my Savior. As my children grew up, they went with me to church until they were eighteen and decided for themselves whether they would go or not.

Still living at home, my nineteen-year-old son got involved with drugs and was arrested. I felt like a knife had gone through my heart and all I wanted to do was hide. I didn't want to attend church where everyone knew what had happened from reading the newspaper.

But the Holy Spirit relentlessly motivated me to go even though I did not want to.

Even when we moved back to my hometown, where few people knew about my son's situation, many Sunday mornings I still wanted to turn the car around and go back home. When my son was arrested a second time, I contacted a prison chaplain who prayed with me and invited me to a prison ministry retreat.

For almost twenty years I have been a part of a prison ministry with women. The Lord brought me through the deepest pain of my life by reminding me to assemble myself together with others in his church.

My family had a habit of reading aloud stories about missionaries. These heroes of the faith set giant examples for me. Hearing of their adventures and incredible sacrifices inspired me and infused me with a desire to be counted among them. Reading the writings of the pillars of the faith nurtured my spiritual growth and expanded the church beyond the building where I occupied a pew.

Our church had co-pastors. Rather than ask the members of the congregation to get behind their church programs, these two men believed that God had called and equipped every person in the church to minister. They encouraged everyone to seek God's direction, then used their position and influence to support each of us. As a result, our church actively ministered in the area prisons, soup kitchens, pregnancy centers, abstinence programs, drug rehabilitation centers, Bible studies, city government, local schools, and hospitals. Our church body was light and salt into our community.

As a teenager, an accident left me paralyzed in the hospital. I was despondent to the point of suicide, but I couldn't even do that for myself. A friend from my church youth group came to visit me. Looking beneath my repulsive appearance, she saw me. She climbed in my bed, held my hand and sang to me, "Man of Sorrows, what a name for the Son of God who came, ruined sinners to reclaim, Hallelujah, what a Savior!" Her touch and her song connected me with Jesus and reminded me that he truly did know what my suffering felt like. Years later, my friend lost her child to death. I telephoned her and sang those same verses to her in her time of deepest pain.

The church is a culmination, the realization of what God had in mind from the beginning.

—PHILIP YANCEY

The Church Discouraged and Discouraging

O Israel, put your hope in the LORD both now and forevermore.

—PSALM 131:3

The Bible tells us to go make *disciples*, not converts to our opinions. Rugged individualism is a trait commonly attributed to American culture. We are a relatively young society and have fought our way from sea to shining sea. Many early frontier settlers were known to move when they could see the light from their neighbor's windows—they felt like civilization was closing in. We value this "me alone against the world" attitude that keeps others at a distance.

This philosophy, which forged America into what it is today, does *not* forge healthy communities of Christian faith. I suppose it is possible to live a Lone Ranger kind of existence, but God created you and me to be social beings with social needs. Romans 12:5 reminds us that we are part of the Church on earth, and as such, "in Christ we who are many form one body, and each member belongs to all the others."

A relationship with Jesus Christ demands *inter*dependence, not independence. Hearing the voice of God happens in the community of believers where it is refined, corrected, and strengthened. It amazes me to meet church friends who are moving, changing jobs, or marrying—and they made that decision all by themselves! People are often proud that they have not conferred with the elders or pastor or another godly person they look up to in the church. Rugged individualism, yes. But not true Christianity. Habits are hard to break.

In *Hearing God's Voice*, Henry and Richard Blackaby wrote, "Hearing God's voice is a community process—not the quest for a personal holy grail. God designed people for interdependence and community. As Christians commit themselves to their fellow believers, God speaks through the church to benefit every member. Estranged from the church, Christians will not hear all God has to say to them."

Burdened with problems great and small, I go to church and then marvel when I leave at the distinct sense I have that God has spoken. I am blessed and relieved. I have perspective again. How did it happen? Was the sermon just for me, answering all my needs? Not always. It is a combination of obedience in being there, strategic conversations with brothers and sisters in Christ, phrases in the hymns and choruses, and the Scriptures brought forward from the pulpit. In the church family I worship with, I know the faith stories of many in the congregation. Just seeing them reminds me of God's faithfulness. Sometimes life is hard and answers are slow in coming. Yet God's ways are inscrutable.

The other, less pleasant side of the coin, is that being a long time in this one-faith family reminds me that "the way of the unfaithful is hard" (Proverbs 13:15) and "a man reaps what he sows" (Galatians 6:7). Both scriptural warnings are written to God's children. At times my living, breathing church family demonstrates bad choices and the resulting long trip home. It is good for my children and me to live alongside and be part of the healing process.

We find ourselves drawn to the church like a moth to a flame. Sometimes we get burned.

—PHIL CALLAWAY

What Others Say about the Church

Feeling that I was not getting any take-home value from regular attendance at church, I was tempted to stop going. Reading through Scripture daily, however, I was impressed by Jesus Christ's example. What could Jesus possibly gain from going to synagogue that he did not already experience in God's presence in Heaven and through his own personal prayer life? The obvious answer is nothing. Jesus attended to give—not to get. Following Jesus Christ's example, I know it is right for me to go to church.

Open about my Christian faith while I held a prominent public position, my family and I felt like we were under a microscope held equally by the liberal left and by the religious right. Everything we did or said was scrutinized. After I retired, my children had a hard time being involved in the church because they felt our family had been ill-treated by fellow conservative believers. Christians can be so busy protecting the church's reputation that we convey judgment and exclusion rather than grace and forgiveness.

Many times I have chafed during the Sunday service, bored and wanting to be about my own agenda. That's when I rein in my wandering thoughts, reminding myself of Acts 20:7, "On the first day of the week we came together to break bread. Paul spoke to the people and, because he intended to leave the next day, kept on talking until midnight." Yikes! I'm thankful my pastor teaches weekly, and his messages fit into a morning time allotment. Then I center my attention back on the service, alert to catch what God would want me to learn about him.

Relocating to a new town, our family settled in at a local church. Immediately several ladies besieged me with "opportunities to minister." As a mother with several young children, I was not in a place to take on the jobs they suggested, nor was I a fit for those ministries. After praying about their requests, I declined the positions. The church ladies stopped talking to me. Later when I offered to serve in other areas, my offer was ignored. It was difficult to enjoy Sunday mornings feeling unaccepted.

Exiled to the island of Patmos, John wrote, "On the Lord's Day I was in the Spirit, and I heard behind me a loud voice like a trumpet" (Revelation 1:10). John considered it important to keep the Lord's Day even while he was in prison. And in that setting, Jesus met John, and John saw Jesus as he had never seen him before.

Jill Briscoe said, "Perhaps it's hard for you to be 'in the Spirit' on the Lord's Day. Maybe you feel like you are on an island, isolated by circumstances, separated against your will from those you love. If you will stay in touch with the God who has allowed these circumstances, you will see Jesus as you have never seen him before. So don't waste the pain.

Suffering helps you see God as you've never seen him before—just as John did. It also helps you see aspects of Jesus' character in a whole new way—just as John did. We can let suffering drive us deeper into God and know that he's waiting."

Some churches are big on Bible studies and deep thinkers. They are weak on applying the Scripture to everyday life. This can make for a weak church that is not growing spiritually, but growing only in knowledge. 1 Corinthians 8:1 says, "Knowledge puffs up, but love builds up." A quote attributed to H. A. Ironside, a well-known Bible teacher of the 1930s and 1940s, says, "They rightly divide the Word of Truth but wrongly divide their own lives."

Daniel in the Old Testament is my example when I am discouraged. He's probably the one person in the Bible who didn't make big mistakes. Despite all kinds of disappointments and challenges, he kept on praying as he was accustomed to doing. He was committed to being faithful to his God. Like Daniel, I want to be faithful in my commitment to the Lord and to my church.

Rather than each family member going to an age-appropriate class, our family preferred to sit together during the Sunday service. Other church members said hurtful remarks like, "What part of our Sunday school program offends you?" "If you think you could run a better program, why don't you do it?" The Sunday school program was terrific, we merely wanted to spend one hour a week being together and learning from the same teacher. Because we were different, others made judgments.

Small groups were the social avenues in our church. With several small children, a traveling spouse, and an already busy calendar, attending a weekly small group in addition to Sunday services was not feasible. Sadly, because I was not part of a small group, I did not receive support during tough times or baby showers to celebrate the good happenings in our family.

A zealous and natural "idea person," I became discouraged when no one at church was getting on board with my great suggestions. Feeling unappreciated, frustrated, and misunderstood, I began to distance myself from the church body. During this time, I read about Peter's similar experience in the New Testament. Peter had a zeal for action and for implementing great plans, but Jesus rebuked Peter for drawing a sword to defend his beloved friend. Like me, Peter felt unappreciated, probably misunderstood. Pursuant to this emotional event, Scripture records that Peter followed Jesus "at a distance." That distance led to Peter's denial of Jesus, and then deep regret. I learned from Peter that distancing myself from my church community and my relationship with Christ is a choice that will certainly lead to regret.

After a humiliating divorce, it was too painful for me to return to the church family. People did not understand my drastic change in status.

After my usual night closing down the local bar, I telephoned an out-of-state friend just to talk. She led me to the Lord over the phone. The next day I found a church and took my place in the front row.

Four weeks later, my four-wheeler broke down so I couldn't drive to church. Though no one from church came to see me, a buddy from the bar stopped by, wondering what had happened to me. Then a woman from the bar came by with a meal, thinking maybe that I was ill since I hadn't been drinking with them for several weeks. She said my friends from the bar offered to buy my beers if I was out of money. I told her that even though no one at the church would sit by me, talk to me, park by me, or come visit me, I was a Christian now.

There were eight churches within one mile of my mother yet no one ever knocked on her door or reached out to her. At forty, she committed suicide. I encourage Christians everywhere to invite a "piece of garbage" into your home for a meal. That piece of garbage might be me.

Having an active baby made church attendance nearly impossible. Getting the baby and myself ready on Sunday morning was exhausting. It was silly to get all dressed up just to spend the morning in the nursery nursing a cranky, sleepy child. Several habits helped me persevere through this season of life. First, the night before church I bathed the baby, prepared the diaper bag, and set out our clothing for the next morning. Second, I set the alarm clock earlier to give me adequate time. Third, I packed quiet snacks and toys. Fourth, my husband and I agreed to take turns caring for the baby during church allowing each of us to really hear the sermon. Fifth, I learned how to sing, pray, and listen to the sermon from the back of the church where I often stood and rocked a cranky child.

Just walking through the church parking lot discouraged me from attending church. Having forgiveness, salvation, and eternal life, Christians should be the happiest people on earth. Yet members of my church were consistently solemn and unfriendly in the parking lot and just as unpleasant inside. There was no motivation to get dressed up and go to a place where people were not happy to see me.

Our church was deficient in training men to lead and lay down their lives in service to their families and the church. On the other hand, the church was quick to assign women to staff the nursery, teach Sunday school, children's church, vacation Bible school, youth programs, and Bible studies, run the missions project, lead the choir, play the piano, produce the newsletter and bulletin, send greeting cards, bring meals, and clean the building. The men were never asked to do anything except approve or disapprove any decision the women made. While the ladies were juggling crying babies, busy toddlers, classes of children, and teaching teenagers, the men enjoyed a quiet hour hearing the sermon, followed by a potluck meal served up by their wives. After tending my own children, home, and extended family needs all week, Sunday was just another exhausting workday.

Hypocrites populated the church in Jesus' day just as today. But that fact didn't keep Jesus away anymore than it should keep me away.

Believers act like unbelievers when they are unwilling to totally commit to a local church. In some ways people treat marriage and church loyalty in similar fashion; they want to be sure there is a handy way out in case something or someone more interesting comes along.

I become discouraged when I compare my meager abilities to the abundant talents of others in the church. Then Scripture reminds me that Abraham and Jacob were liars, Moses stuttered and had outbursts of anger, David had an affair, Jeremiah was depressed, Hosea's wife was unfaithful, Naomi was a widow, Jonah ran away from God, Paul was a murderer, and Timothy probably had ulcers. God even used Balaam's donkey. If God could use them, he can use me. Patsy Clairmont expressed it best when she said, "God uses cracked pots and I'm the visual aid."

Luis Palau and his evangelistic team were in Scotland years ago, holding evangelistic meetings in many small towns. Discouraged by the lack of response to one evening's altar call, the men on the team began the drive back to Aberdeen. The gloomy, cold, stiff atmosphere matched their mood. Because of the late hour, the only option for eating was a roadside pub. They parked and cautiously walked into the warm and noisy establishment. "Hey, you chaps look like Americans," someone welcomed and bought them a round of soft drinks. Over a hot meal, the team members had the opportunity to talk about spiritual matters with people who were interested. As the team drove away, they could not help but make an obvious comparison.

Once upon a time, a Babylonian king gave an edict to humanity, either go to build God's temple or give so someone else could go. His name was Cyrus and the edict is in the first chapter of the book of Ezra. His superior made a similar edict five hundred years later, "Go into all the world . . . build my Church . . . give to the poor." This month I will be taking my son and a couple from my church to resource and serve a dozen churches in the poorest of the Asian nations. There are whole churches without a musical instrument, and pastors without study Bibles. On my last visit to the Philippines I saw a church planted and many pastors supplied with study tools.

My lifelong relationship with the church has taught me two things. First, human nature is not a pretty sight. Second, sometimes people rise to leadership in the church though they do not possess a living, vital relationship with Jesus Christ. These leaders may have leadership skills and a desire to lead, but spiritually have only head knowledge of the Christian faith. This leadership occurs in a vacuum, similar to the Old Testament story of the Israelites who demanded a king to rule over them. Saul became their first king, but his relationship with God was an intellectual one, not a heart relationship.

> *As a boy of twelve, Jesus had said to his parents, who had been looking for he, "You should have known that I would be in my Father's house" (Luke 2:49, NLT). Years later he taught in the synagogues (see Luke 4:14, 15). When he went to his hometown, Nazareth, "he went as usual to the synagogue on the Sabbath" (Luke 4:16 NLT).*
>
> *We will never find a perfect church, and if we do, we should be careful not to join it, lest we spoil it! We should make our presence felt in our church!*
>
> *Fellowship is a very important part of our spiritual life, for it keeps our faith burning. If a coal falls out of a fire, it will soon go out. Believers need to be an active part of a local church. As we focus individually and collectively on God's things, God is pleased.*
>
> —JILL BRISCOE

The Church—My Home

In this world the sheep are often scattered, but in every true member of the Church there is a homing instinct and a longing for a fold and a shepherd.

—CHURCH BULLETIN

Church is one of the few places where we leave better than when we entered.

—VICTOR PARACHIN

Why are we attracted to a particular church? Americans usually say it is the church's theology, the church's government, or the church's programs. But to some degree we like a particular church simply because of the temperament God gave us—how we're wired to approach people and ideas.

Most of us choose a church based on the personality of the congregation and leadership. We congregate where things are done somewhat the way our minds work. As I learned in missionary training, these distinctives are not wrong, just different. It is often a matter of taste.

Christians have big theological arguments about why one denomination is more correct than another one, but the true body of Christ exists with a variety of distinctives. That we have so many denominations is nothing to be ashamed of. It is a tremendous demonstration of the creativity of God. We don't have to do the details exactly the same way as long as God is the center of our worship.

Churches differ in forms of church government, styles of worship, offices of leadership, how an offering is taken or not taken, the practice of baptism and communion, and even what terminology is used. None of these things is "to die for," but we can be amazingly slow to adapt to any practice or Bible translation that is different from what we are used to.

My husband and I attend the church that has been my home for nearly sixty years. I came as a very small child! I have observed generations before me, with me, and in front of me live their lives in this local family called Cedar Mill Bible Church. On Sundays I greet old friends, their children, their children's children, and meet newcomers. I come to worship God, encourage his children, and be challenged by his preached Word. Together we observe communion.

Union and Communion

One distinctive of my church is that we take communion weekly—and it has never been boring. When I arrive, dragging the week's successes and failures along with me, I am desperate for silence. In celebrating the Lord's Supper, I deal with whatever it is that has caused that quietness to leave. I think about Jesus on the cross dealing with my sin and suddenly everything else settles out and makes sense.

There is no issue in the Christian experience that is not dealt with during communion. The Lord's Supper reminds me that Jesus Christ died my death, took my sins, rose from the dead, and brought me forgiveness. It is my opportunity to leave the failures, through confession, at the foot of the cross before the burden and guilt becomes deeply entrenched and permeates other aspects of my life and relationships. Communion helps us keep short accounts in our secret, private lives.

Communion visibly reminds us of what Jesus Christ did for us. Different from each other, we bring the baggage of our fallenness, memories of what was, or regret for what might have been. As we gather together around the Lord's

Table, Jesus says, "do this in remembrance of me" (Luke 22:19). We lift our eyes from selfish concerns and worries to rejoice that we are part of such an imperfect but redeemed family because of Christ. Every week we can evaluate, confess sin, receive forgiveness, renew right perspectives, and begin again. How much we miss if we neglect the assembling of ourselves together—particularly to celebrate the Lord's Supper. It is health for our souls.

The Lord's Supper reminds us that the ground is level at the foot of the cross. Each time I take the bread and the cup in my hand, I look over the congregation. We eat together. We all belong. We are alike in that we have a common Lord and a common trust in Jesus Christ for our salvation. How different from other associations where people scramble for leadership, respect, or position. (It can happen in the church, but God forbid that it should.) In the church, "There is neither Jew nor Greek, slave nor free, male nor female, for you are all one in Christ Jesus" (Galatians 3:28).

In my ministry, I spend time with women who have unfortunate issues in their pasts, things they've done or had done to them. They agonize over the God that would receive them on a level playing field with everyone else when they feel inferior to others in the church family.

Through unwise choices, one woman found herself divorced with a small child. Haunted by her past, she felt she was somehow on a lower track in the church and thus unusable to God. One day the Holy Spirit penetrated the memories of her past. At last she understood that she was forgiven, accepted, and loved—just like the rest of us. Hebrews 10:17 reads, "Their sins and lawless acts I will remember no more." When she understood that God's grace is a gift, she was changed. Her choices changed, her appearance changed, she looked her peers in the eye and became a challenging, strong friend.

The local church exemplifies the love of God for his children. It doesn't matter if you call it communion or the Eucharist or the Breaking of Bread. Celebrating the Lord's Supper together tangibly reminds us that we are all one, all the same, equally gifted and loved, with equal access to God.

> *I wanted to know everything about Bill so I was delighted when his mother asked if I wanted to look through his family scrapbooks. To know God and the life of Christ, we must study the Bible. We must read God's Word so we know if a ministry is valid.*
>
> —GLORIA GAITHER

What Others Say about the Church

As a pastor, I request that people who are considering attending this church visit at least three times. I would not want anyone to judge the church based on an "off" Sunday anymore than I would want him or her to judge the church based on a great Sunday. Pray about the church home the Lord would have you be a part of, and visit potential congregations at least three times before crossing them off your list.

My children had been attending a Bible study through a local church that sent a van around to pick them up. When my life and marriage fell apart, I got in the van, too. That church became my family.

The strength of our church is in following the practice of the biblical Bereans. Members are encouraged to compare everything that is heard from the pulpit with what the Bible says. Leadership focuses on nourishing the people with the Word of God according to 1 Corinthians 4:6, which says, "Do not go beyond what is written."

A faltering economy caused the public schools in our area to cut back on needed maintenance, grounds keeping, and janitorial tasks. Four groundskeepers were assigned to maintain ninety-eight campuses. Several churches adopted nearby schools by cutting the grass, weeding flower beds, painting, and doing various repairs. In a single Saturday, the many church members who came out to work refreshed a tired, worn-out school campus. The church eased the burden of overloaded administrators and served as a caring segment of the community.

I grew up in a family characterized by competition, judgment, rivalry, and criticism. When I began attending a church characterized by grace, I felt like I had finally come home.

Every week after Sunday service, our church has a potluck lunch. Birthdays for the week are celebrated with a rousing chorus of *Happy Birthday*. Anniversaries, graduations, and other newsworthy items are announced. It is a time of coming together, fellowship, and building a network within the church body. Everyone brings a dish for the table, provides their own table service, and people take turns setting up and cleaning up. This time has become a highlight because it knits our hearts together and provides every participant with a sense of belonging.

"If you don't come apart . . . you will come apart," our pastor says. He and his wife get away for a respite every quarter. When a church member experiences a significant change in life, such as a marriage, pregnancy, birth of a child, or death of a loved one, a deacon telephones to offer a break from whatever ministry responsibilities that person has. It is a thoughtful way to come alongside one another.

My dad was in the military so our family relocated often. Finding a church was first priority in each new home. Our family looked for a healthy spiritual atmosphere consisting of six aspects: (1) the church honored Jesus Christ in its overall ministry, (2) all members of our family were able to participate in worship and activities, (3) intentional teaching instructed all ages how to do the right thing in every area of life, (4) youth groups were founded on strong principles of godly behavior, (5) leadership was united and cooperative, and (6) questions concerning faith were welcomed.

I'm thankful for the many artistic and creative expressions of the faith exhibited in our church. Those expressions include music, drama, testimony, service, ritual, prayers, architecture, and creeds. Each member of my large family is touched by a different part of the service. My artistic child benefits from the music and drama, my auditory learner appreciates the sermon, my doer enjoys service projects, and my social person grows through regular fellowship with other believers.

I leave Sunday worship service better than when I entered. The sermon, music, Scripture readings, prayer, and fellowship encourage me to make needed changes in my attitude and behavior.

We all experience crises in life, what Ephesians 6:13 calls "the day of evil." It is a day or period of time when things don't go well. Attacks come from within and without. In those rugged times, we are told in Ephesians 6:14 to "stand firm." Ecclesiastes 12:1 says, "Remember your Creator in the days of your youth, before the days of trouble come and the years approach when you will say, 'I find no pleasure in them.'" Being involved in a local congregation is our support against and during "the day of evil."

My wife and I are part of a small missions-oriented fellowship. They "get it" in terms of our peculiar needs as parents of overseas missionaries.

Coming from a non-Christian biological family, my church family is vital to my faith. Sundays are weekly mini-family reunions with my spiritual family. Prayer meetings, Bible studies, potlucks, and fellowship activities fuel me to keep on going and growing.

Our diverse congregation worked because we banded together to reach the community around us. The church sponsored programs that taught people how to read, offered free tax and legal aid, counseling, and assistance for single mothers and their children. A ministry provided food and social activities for seniors. Serving others caused us to think less about ourselves. When looking for a church, look for one that focuses on reaching outward.

According to Barna Research, these ten critical factors keep members and visitors attending church on a regular basis:

1. Theological beliefs and doctrine
2. How much the people care about each other
3. Quality of sermons
4. Friendliness
5. Involvement in serving the poor and disadvantaged
6. The quality of the programs and classes for children
7. How much the person liked the pastor
8. The denominational affiliation of the church
9. Quality of the adult Sunday school classes
10. Convenience of the weekend service times

The local church is the hope of the world.

— CARL PALMER, Teaching Pastor
Cedar Mill Bible Church

The Church Where
I Belong

*Now you are the body of Christ, and each one of
you is a part of it. And in the church God has
appointed first of all apostles, second prophets, third
teachers, then workers of miracles, also those having
gifts of healing, those able to help others, those with
gifts of administration, and those speaking in different kinds of tongues.*

—1 CORINTHIANS 12:27, 28

Church buildings come in a variety of shapes and
sizes. The architectural style of a church building
may even indicate what denomination meets inside.
Think of the many words used to describe the place of

worship—assembly, chapel, church, fellowship, Gospel hall, house of God, synagogue, sanctuary, temple, worship center. Whether we gather in a hut or a stained glass structure, there is creative variety in what happens when we are together.

As a child I was told not to run around in the church. Adults quoted Habakkuk 2:20, "But the LORD is in his holy temple; let all the earth be silent before him," which meant all us restless children were to keep quiet in God's house. Later congregational wisdom refined the thought, *"I am the temple of God,"* to give priority to our spiritual lives over physical buildings. (Still, our children do need reminding that any public building demands our best behavior! When I was a guest at the White House, I took great care to conform to custom in what I wore and how quietly I spoke.)

God does not exclusively inhabit the dusty old church of my childhood. He lives in people and we gather to worship in a convenient place. Buildings are varied, but not useless—we are physical beings who take up space and inhabit time. We need a place in which we can come together.

There is also a fine line between giving a building "airs" it cannot possibly fulfill and underestimating the blessing that a local familiar gathering place represents. After 9/11, people had an urgency to pray *in* a church. I remind myself that God also hears my mumbled plea for help as I drive to an appointment. I doubt the Trinity cares much whether we sit cross-legged on the ground, on separate sides for men and women, use instruments to sing, pray from a formulated book, or participate in a program that has no visible plan.

The Lord is pleased by our hunger and effort to be together with brothers and sisters in Christ, and he is pleased when we worship him. Getting together is for our well-being, but ultimately it is for him who deserves all our attention, praise, and worship. I am convinced that it is impossible to meet together and honestly say, "I got absolutely nothing out of that." I don't believe it. You weren't trying. No hymn, Scripture, prayer, conversation, memory? Really! As long as I'm alive and kicking, church is serious business and is always worth the effort.

The wonderful New Testament truth is that when we leave that building, whatever we call it, as believers and disciples of Christ Jesus, we take him with us!

When we are looking for a church fellowship to join—and we should—we should ask if it teaches that Jesus died and rose again and that he is the only way to heaven. We should inquire if it teaches that the Bible is the inspired word of God. We must study the Scriptures, and compare what is being taught with what we have studied (see Acts 17:10–12).

Growing in Christ means that we will become pro-
ductive and useful (see 2 Peter 1:8)—we will
begin to exhibit the character qualities of Christ's
disciple (see 2 Peter 1:5–7). We can ask God to
teach us more about himself. Then we will be able to
discern truth from error and can join a church that
teaches the Bible accurately and well.

—JILL BRISCOE

What Others Say about the Church

Psalm 61:5 reads, "You have given me the heritage of those who fear your name." My earthly heritage is not impressive. As far as I know I come from a long line of unbelievers, some of whom were great sinners like me. But God, by his great grace and mercy, has given me the spiritual heritage of all those who fear his name. My true heritage is with Abraham, David, Daniel, Paul, Billy Graham, the Palaus, and all those who love and follow Jesus. My family is the family of God. What an amazing gift.

I made a commitment to go to church regularly. When I feel like staying home, that is Satan working to give me an excuse. Church is a place of solace and comfort, the place where I come to worship the Lord with fellow Christians when I know others in the world don't have that freedom. My role is to not forsake the fellowship of other believers. If my feelings are so centered on myself, I will be hurt by whatever others say. If I am focused on Jesus Christ, people can walk on top of me with cleats and I won't even feel it. If every time someone hurts my feelings, I get offended and stop going to church, how many times would I change churches?

Now that my children are grown, my role is to be an encouraging older woman in the church, teaching the younger women about their marriages and families. I pray about my areas of involvement and marvel at the way the Lord equips me to do what I never dreamed I would do, such as teaching an adult Sunday school class filled with students who have college degrees while I only have a high school diploma. I even accepted an acting role in the church Christmas play and was surprised to find that my participation was challenging, fun, and beneficial to the production.

Our large church surveyed the congregation and discovered that the average person felt comfortable attending church once a month. That was enough to make them feel part of the church family. Recently I turned to greet the couple sitting next to me in the worship service. "Have you been here long?" I asked. "Yes, and no," the woman replied. "We've been coming off and on for seven years. We prefer to remain under the radar screen." I wanted to tell them about the benefits they lose and the growth they will not experience, but I held my tongue.

In the same way the Old Testament priest's garment carried the representation of the twelve tribes before the Lord's remembrance each time he entered the Lord's presence, I bring my church, family, community, and world regularly before the Lord's remembrance in prayer. Being a faithful prayer warrior is my most important job.

The local congregation is a helpful resource in the raising of our children, a backdrop of support and encouragement. Ultimately it is the parent's responsibility to instill values, a hunger to know God personally, and a thirst for closeness to Jesus. The church partners with parents as we nurture our children spiritually. When our children reach out in a time of guilt, confusion, failure, or need of any kind, we trust they will seek spiritual assistance from those properly gifted in the comfort of the church they know and where they are known.

When my spouse and I were first married, we moved to a small town. We began attending a church where we felt we could help with the youth ministry. There are not a lot of churches in our county and, though rather small, our church is a tool to help us reach our town for Jesus. I have friends who do not see the need to commit themselves to a local body of believers. They are missing so much. We need to be Jesus Christ's hands and feet in our local community.

My husband was one of several military personnel in our church deployed during the war on terrorism. The church supported our families by providing a Saturday morning program for our children that allowed me time to get errands and appointments accomplished quickly. Volunteers helped with house and yard maintenance during that time, too.

It is good for my spirit to attend church weekly where my world is expanded as I am led in worship and taught by others. Hearing how other believers struggled, grew, and lived out their faith inspires my own spiritual walk.

In age, my pastor is "over the hill" but his outlook is fresh. Seeing humor in things keeps him from taking life too seriously. He is focused on the health of our local congregation, not distracted by desires to be recognized on a grander scale. He takes care of himself physically to be in the best shape to continue to minister for the Lord. He has set an admirable pace that the rest of us are inspired to follow. In exchange, we as the church body realize he is on the front lines spiritually. Whenever he looks back over his shoulder, he sees us praying faithfully for him.

I can do more to help others when I am involved in a local church than I can do by myself. Those of us in the church come together to better feed the hungry, clothe

the unclothed, and help the hurting. When two or more of us gather together, Jesus Christ is in the midst of us and our labors are multiplied.

Visiting a new church can feel awkward. To help visitors feel comfortable, I greet each one, invite them to a Sunday school class, and frequently take them to lunch. During the week, I follow up with a phone call or bring a potted plant to their home. I read an encouraging Scripture, pray for their household, and invite them to come again.

> *The world's a better place because Michelangelo*
> *   didn't say, "I don't do ceilings."*
> *The world's a better place because a German*
> *   monk named Martin Luther didn't say,*
> *   "I don't do doors."*
> *The world's a better place because an Oxford*
> *   don named John Wesley didn't say, "I don't*
> *   do fields."*
> *The world's a better place because Moses didn't say,*
> *   "I don't do Pharaohs."*
> *The world's a better place because Noah didn't say,*
> *   "I don't do arks and animals."*
> *The world's a better place because Ruth didn't say,*

"I don't do mothers-in-law."
The world's a better place because Mary didn't say,
   "I don't do virgin births."
The world's a better place because Mary Magdalene
   didn't say, "I don't do feet."
The world's a better place because Jesus didn't say,
   "I don't do crosses."

—LEONARD SWEET,
   A Cup of Coffee at the Soul Cafe

The Church— Home for Our Children

Passing on Our Faith

Dear Lord,
I do not ask
That thou shouldst give me some high work of thine.
Some noble calling, or some wondrous task.
Give me a little hand to hold in mine.
Give me a little child to point the way
Over the strange, sweet path that leads to Thee.
Give me a little voice to teach to pray,
Give me the shining eyes Thy face to see.
The only crown I ask, dear Lord, to wear
Is this: that I may teach a little child.
I do not ask that I may ever stand
Among the wise, the worthy, or the great;
I only ask that softly, hand in hand,
A child and I may enter at the Gate.

—AUTHOR UNKNOWN

As a parent, or grandparent, you can set in motion spiritual dynamics that could impact your family for generations to come. The local church helps you all along the way.

When I was a child, our nondenominational congregation was the center of my life. I could walk the half-mile to the church. The building was a revived pioneer structure with two rooms, a steeple, and a wood-burning stove that had to be stoked in the winter. Like a picture postcard, there was an add-on back room for the youngest children's Sunday school. The rest of us made the best of Sunday school classes consisting of two pews and a teacher holding forth as best as he could.

I confess there were occasional Sundays when I participated in a silent game of shoving the next person on the bench. Just a little, then a little bit more, until the young scholar on the end of the bench fell off. Despite the dull mumbling of other classes within earshot, we did learn from the lesson. Each week I carried home Sunday school papers from the curriculum we were studying.

Then my church moved down the road and built a building with real classrooms and indoor toilets. A sanctuary was added in time for my marriage in the early 1960s. The congregation is now enjoying worship center number four.

My parents followed a pretty set pattern on Sundays. We all went to Sunday school, followed by Sunday worship service. I recall being extremely hungry if the service went extra long. Sunday dinner was a meal left to cook slowly in the oven and my parents often spontaneously invited someone home to share it with us.

Father always observed a Sunday nap on the living room couch. No exceptions. Children eyeballing him relentlessly, looking for signs that he was waking up did not move him. When he woke, we children began pestering him for a ride to the park or to visit friends. Can you imagine stopping by someone's house for a spontaneous visit today? Visiting friends was a great Sunday activity. Being a civil engineer, my father frequently favored a jaunt to look at some past or future road-building project. The highlight for us children was the traditional stop at Dairy Queen for ice cream. We either went back to church for the evening service or we played games at home.

Sunday Memories

Growing up in Argentina, Luis Palau recalls that playing, or listening to, soccer games was proper on weekdays but prohibited on Sundays. Childhood Sundays for Luis were full days of rigorous routine. The family rose early to be at church for the Lord's Supper at 9:00 A.M., followed by Sunday school. In the afternoons, the family engaged in evangelism on the street corners, children's classes in their garage, or visiting the sick. Someone would haul out the harmonium (a shrill-sounding pedal organ) and Luis' mother led a rousing hymn. Luis tried to help with the music by playing the accordion until he realized that the Holy Spirit distributes the gifts—and music was not one of his! After an evening service in the tiny chapel at 8:00 P.M., everyone who considered themselves part of the youth group gathered in a home for singing, teaching, and fun.

Luis remembers Sunday as a day of worship and service, but not as a chore. In church he learned to preach and teach. The dusty streets, the walk to church with Bibles under their arms in a society where most residents were not headed for worship, all made Luis and his family feel privileged, and occasionally ostracized.

I have a few memories of my own child-rearing and Sundays that keep me from self-righteous lectures to the younger set of parents. One particular Sunday, when all four sons were small, someone spilled orange juice when our family was already running late. Dad was in the car and I could hear little voices chirping, "Hurry up, Mom."

"Why, in the division of labors, do all the fun jobs come my way?" I steamed to myself as I sponged up the worst of the dripping, sticky mess.

No preplanning can prevent all the last moment surprises. Satan's little gremlins like nothing better than to hide a small child's shoe so that the family piles into the station wagon or minivan in an unworshipful state.

"I will build my church," said Jesus. Today I see people across the church aisle that I have known all my life. I see a family where God has rebuilt lives and each consecutive generation exhibits more visible success. Another family struggles to hold on in spite of disappointment and health issues, victories and defeats. Those of us who have found Jesus Christ as Savior will someday be the focus of a memorial service when we move on to our real home.

When babies are dedicated or baptized, we as a congregation are reminded of our responsibility to pray for, teach, and encourage the child and the parents in their spiritual growth. We are a spiritual family.

As a church family we partake of the Lord's Supper and sing, "My Jesus I love thee, I know thou art mine. . . ." How many years has it been? My heart still trembles at the weakness and failure I see in my own life. "Would He devote that sacred head for such a worm as I?" Yes, he would.

I see his strong hand disciplining, comforting, encouraging, and sometimes using me in the process as he ministers to my church family. Church is a vital spiritual tradition until the number of my days on earth is fulfilled and he comes to take me home.

Prayer for Our Children

Father, hear us, we are praying,
Hear the words our hearts are saying,
We are praying for our children—
Keep them from the powers of evil,
From the secret hidden peril,
Father, hear us for our children—
From the whirlpool that would suck them,
From the treacherous quicksand pluck them,
Father hear us for our children—
From the worldling's hollow gladness,
From the sting of faithless sadness,
Father, Father, keep our children—
Through life's troubled waters steer them,
Through life's bitter battle cheer them,
Father, Father, be thou near them—
Read the language of our longing,
Read the wordless pleadings thronging,
Holy Father, for our children—
And wherever they may bide,
Lead them Home at eventide.

—AMY CARMICHAEL

What Others Say about the Church

As an eight-year-old watching the lives of my class-mates, soccer team members, and neighborhood play-mates, I often asked my parents if someone was a Christian. Mom and Dad consistently replied, "We don't know. Just because a person goes to a particular church does not mean that you or I can decide whether they are a true follower of Jesus Christ. Only God knows their hearts." Now an adult, I still see people judging another's spirituality by the company they keep. Church attendance has become a type of thermometer we use on one another. My parents used our drive time to talk about God's boundless grace and his exclusive knowl-edge of the heart. When we get to heaven I think we shall be somewhat surprised by who is there and who is not. First Samuel 16:7 says, "The LORD does not look at the things man looks at. Man looks at the outward appearance, but the LORD looks at the heart."

The best thing my parents did to pass their faith on to me was to stay committed to their marriage vows. It takes two to make a good marriage, and Mom and Dad each did their best to live out the biblical principles of treating the other with honor and respect. Their marriage was faith in action.

The Old Testament priest Eli raised his sons in the house of God, but they did not follow God. Samuel grew up in the Tabernacle but that did not guarantee a relationship with God until God called him. As a parent I tried to set the stage for my children to hear and respond when God called them. I prayed daily that my children would belong to the Lord. I taught them God's principles found in Scripture, studied Christian books with them, and filled our home with music that praised the Lord. Church attendance and serving within the church was a regular part of our lives. I did my part to see that my children grew up in the presence of the Lord so they would recognize his voice when he called them to himself.

Committed to our local church, my parents passed on the importance of fellowship with believers, corporate worship, and serving. They taught Sunday school, Pioneer programs, and served on the deacon board. We often had missionaries in our home for dinner and to stay the night. My parents consistently lived their faith at home.

Though I would not have volunteered for the scenario of living in a household with three teenagers a second time around, it turned out to be a blessing in disguise. Circumstances dictated that my daughter and her teens returned home to live with us. This adjustment occurred at the same time that my husband of fifty-four years required my full-time care. My outings included the medical clinic, the emergency room, and church. What fun to be part of my grandchildren's festive moments and a privilege to share with them from my experiences of a lifetime lived with Jesus Christ. All three of the in-house grandkids love the Lord deeply and serve him in different ways and with a gusto I only imagined when I was their age. The teens pack every moment with mission trips, youth group activities, and friendships. Our multigenerational home has enriched our love for each other and for our common Lord.

Our family treasured Sunday morning worship, Sunday evening service, and Wednesday evening service. My siblings are I are all grown now, but as children we bypassed the children's church programs so we could sit with Dad and Mom in Bible study and prayer meeting.

Dad or Mom's arm was always around my shoulders. I still remember what I learned during those sessions, and those hours together became precious, uninterrupted family time.

Weekly, my youth pastor sent encouraging e-mails to me and the other teens in our youth group. The church staff provided regular opportunities for me to support and participate in mission projects. These two things helped my faith grow.

Mom and Dad were consistent in living by biblical standards all week long, not just on Sunday. They tried to make decisions based on what was pleasing to the Lord. Because they sought to live biblically, I could count on them and that helped me learn that I could count on God. Their everyday walk with God provided peace and security for our family and reinforced my belief in following Jesus Christ.

Dad and Mom had a heart for missions. Every missionary who came into the area was invited to dinner at our home. What a terrific education I received sitting at the table and listening to missionaries tell their stories of the work being done on the mission field. My parents faithfully supported missionaries, and each year our vacation involved a short-term mission trip. This heritage taught me that the church is worldwide and not separated by denominational differences.

I still remember the Sunday morning when my mom "lost it." Dad was away on business and Mom was busy getting all of us children ready for church. Ranging in age from ten to seventeen, several of us kids were grumbling about having to go to church in the first place. That's when our even-tempered, sweet-talking mom announced that she wrapped her life around us, did what we wanted year in and year out, listened to our music, slaved for us all week long, cooked our food, cleaned up after us, did our laundry, helped with our homework, and got us to all our extracurricular activities. The only thing she wanted was a peaceful, blessed time of worshiping the Lord on a Sunday, so it was time for us to simmer down, and get in the car without one whine out of anybody. It made a strong impact on me that my mom felt so passionately about attending church.

As a church-grown kid, I had to transition from my parents' faith to develop a faith of my own. To aid that process, my parents didn't make church attendance a condition of living at home. If I didn't want to go to church or if I wanted to sleep in on Sunday mornings, they suggested that I focus on my personal relationship with God by reading the Bible and praying later in the day. My parents thought it was important to attend church, but didn't insist that I attend their church. They allowed me to attend other Christian churches and camps with my friends from high school. We were a prominent family in our congregation so my sporadic attendance did not reflect well on them. During high school and independent of my family, my faith became my own.

The number of folks who come to church only when it is convenient surprises me. Christian parents raised me and we went to church and Sunday school every week. When our family went on vacation, we visited churches wherever we went. It broadened my view of the body of Christ to meet other Christians in other areas, to worship with them, and to see how others "do church." As an adult, I continue the tradition. Whenever

I am out of town on business, I attend church where I am. I have attended big churches and small ones, famous ones and unknown congregations. What a sweet fellowship to be with spiritual brothers and sisters no matter where I go.

My siblings and I often embarrassed my parents in church with our green or purple hair, pierced body parts, and unusual clothes. We didn't look like perfect church kids, but our parents knew that our faith was genuine and our actions were a healthy expression of growing up. My parents viewed appearance as secondary to character and they valued us above their reputation or what other people thought.

I will never forget the Sunday a missionary finished giving his message to the congregation and then specifically sought out my dad. The missionary warmly grasped my dad's big, work-worn hand and thanked Dad for his faithful financial support over the past couple years. The missionary explained that the work had been especially difficult in a primitive foreign country. In addition, the financial support others had pledged had been sporadic and in many cases had ceased. "Except for you," the missionary said. "When I felt discouraged, your faithful and timely support arrived each month like clockwork." Previously I had viewed my dad's plodding ways with disdain. That Sunday, and without words of his own, my dad taught me the value of consistency and the power of faithful support.

When I protested about going to church, my parents made a point of listening to my reasons for not wanting to attend. The trade-off was that we talked about it after church, not while we were getting ready to leave on Sunday morning. My complaints centered around feeling insignificant, feeling like no one liked me, feeling that the youth leaders had favorites, and that church in general was boring. Since staying home was not an option, we worked together to find a solution. Dad explained that teachers who are nervous about teaching favor those who make them feel confident. Teachers changed with the passing quarters or years, and my parents assured me that adults faced the same situations. We decided to value everyone's answers in our Sunday school classes, and to speak encouraging words to those we attended church with. We agreed that church was a place to join and serve. My parents challenged me to be part of the solution rather than simply complain about the problems.

My earliest childhood memories are of sitting on my mother's lap during church service. There were no alternatives such as junior church, children's classes, or nursery care. Children sat with their parents. Even while quietly squirming around on the floor underneath the pew, I learned a lot of things from the sermon. My ears perked up whenever the pastor told a story.

Dad and Mom set the alarm clock to wake us in plenty of time to get ready for church without feeling rushed and cranky. Because church was important to them, it naturally became important to us children. Friends frequently came over after church for a meal, and visitors and newcomers were also invited. An occasional new outfit made me eager to go to church so I could wear my new duds. Since Sunday was a special day for our family, and our special day centered around church, going to church has easily become a favored part of my week as an adult.

I have no greater joy than to hear that my children are walking in the truth.

—3 JOHN 4

A Church for the Struggling

For my beloved I will not fear
Love knows what to do, for him, for her
From year to year, as hitherto;
Whom my heart cherishes are dear
To Thy heart too.

—AMY CARMICHAEL

The Christian life is not a hundred-yard dash, but a slow, steady walk. Legalism and silly prohibitions within a spiritual community often prove to be obstacles to faith. Sometimes the daily struggles or the terrible tragedies of life cripple us, and we have difficulty even reaching out to the church for help. Additionally, the accelerating pace of life nibbles at God's plan for the day set apart to celebrate Jesus Christ's resurrection.

What about Hypocrites?

A part of Scotland noted for strict Sabbath restrictions—including prohibitions against reading the paper or wiggling on Sunday—circulated this story: A young lad entered a seedy hotel with his arm around the local village lady of the night. As they climbed the stairs to a rented room, the young man began to whistle. Instantly, the lass stopped and turned to her companion. "I'll have you to know I shall not sleep with a man who whistles on the Sabbath!"

Extreme, of course, but in between the extremes are gains and losses. No one desires to return to a system of pointless inactivity as though God demanded it. That is legalism.

The church is full of hypocrites, individuals who pretend to be something they are not. I fit that definition. So did the apostle Paul, who admitted, "For what I want to do I do not do, but what I hate I do" (Romans 7:15). Hypocrisy is in the eye of the beholder. It is subjective—a judgment call without definitive criterion. There are hypocrites in *every* other sphere of life, so why not in the church where there is hope for change? "I have met the enemy and they are us," Pogo said. The hypocrites Jesus condemned were the religious leaders who laid down rules they themselves would not follow. He never used the word to describe the weakest of his followers or his disciples.

What about Quarrels?

It's not a matter of *if*, but *when* quarrels arise. Usually they revolve around strong personalities who attempt to tie their issues to biblical doctrine, when the real root of the problem is often one of power and control. Scripture emphasizes that leaders are shepherds, characterized by gentleness, who care for the flock. Order is built on looking at our Master and following his style of servant-leadership.

A professor at Wheaton College challenged his students to identify the biblical truths that are worth dying for. If the church limited conflict to those essential teachings—the deity of Jesus Christ, his work on the cross, the authenticity of Scripture, and our need for repentance—then church government, modes of baptism, and other frequently controversial issues that generate more heat than light would not make the cut.

In cultures where the Church is under persecution, there is little fussing over minutia. People with divergent backgrounds join hands to follow Jesus Christ simply and at great cost. Church history reveals how humans squabble over methods and styles century after century. Yet God still loves us and remains committed to us. Jesus said, "I will build my church" (Matthew 16:18) and he has done so with the likes of you and me—in spite of us, not because of us.

Thankfully, Sundays can be refreshing days spent leaving behind the duties, worries, and projects that fill the week. An unhurried morning at church invested in worship, learning, exhortation, meeting friends, encouraging the weak and discouraged, praying together for the Church universal and local, is a Sunday celebration to anticipate.

> *But you have come to Mount Zion, to the heavenly Jerusalem, the city of the living God. You have come to thousands upon thousands of angels in joyful assembly, to the church of the firstborn, whose names are written in heaven. You have come to God, the judge of all men, to the spirits of righteous men made perfect, to Jesus the mediator of a new covenant, and to the sprinkled blood that speaks a better word than the blood of Abel.*
>
> —HEBREWS 12:22–24

What Others Say about the Church

I literally grew up "in the church." Always in church for one activity or another, my parents attended endless committee meetings, but I rarely saw a relationship with Jesus Christ in their daily lives. They would go to church

Sunday morning and have "roast preacher" for lunch as they criticized the sermon, complained about the church programs, and grumbled about who attended. Conflict with other church members was common. Their negative Christianity turned me off and I drifted away from the faith as an adult. It took me some time to separate their sour spirit toward the church from the relevance of Jesus Christ in my own life. I had to sort this all out as an adult.

I expected people in the church to be different. I went to church seeking wisdom in the areas of relationships, finances, marriage, and family. I discovered Christians lived in strife with one another, were often in debt, and Christian marriages were breaking up just as frequently as the unchurched marriages. I wondered what was different, or better, about being a Christian compared to being a non-Christian.

When I was grounded as a teenager, my parents curtailed my social activities and required my attendance at Sunday school, Bible study, prayer meeting, and youth group. I know that my parents meant well but I learned to associate going to church with being punished.

As an adult, I stopped attending church because I didn't immediately find a good church home nearby, and my work and making money became my number one priority.

My past was riddled with abuse. The church I began attending focused on my need to forgive the perpetrator and give up my bitterness. For me, this was impossible. I had been victimized and wounded, and now the church insisted I do the hard work of forgiving. It was all I could do to survive; I had no strength left to tackle the Herculean task of forgiving such an evil violation and destruction of my life. Church became another place where I just did not measure up, where I could not meet the requirements.

I was ready to leave when the leaders in my church sought counsel from another pastor experienced in similar situations. He recommended the leaders listen to me without interruption and then validate my pain and emotions. The church members who were working with me stopped insisting I forgive and instead extended love and compassion. Amazingly, this process of acceptance and empathy allowed me to heal surrounded by safe and accepting Christians. Forgiveness came naturally after both God and his people simply loved me.

In my experience, answered prayer was abundant for me as a new believer but decreased as I matured. Prayer is about changing me through perseverance, being Christ-like, and clinging to God's comfort and strength. Prayer is not about changing my circumstances. True trust is about ruthlessly trusting when I least understand God's ways. Being in a church, surrounded by other mature believers, helped me understand this transition between being a new believer and becoming a person of mature faith.

Located in the inner city, our church noticed that many in the neighborhood felt uncomfortable coming to worship because they did not have nice clothes. The church decided to dress casually so that anyone who came would not feel out of place.

I lead a women's Bible study in my community where one woman faithfully attended for several years. I didn't ask where she attended church and she never said. One day after class she thanked me for all she had learned and the blessing that the group had been to her. She told me her husband was retiring and they were relocating. "This Bible study has been my church," she explained. "My husband is not a believer and he always has something he wants to do on Sundays. Through this study my faith has grown and been encouraged." I realized that day that there are people who must creatively find ways to worship, have fellowship, and "do church."

Hypocrisy in our youth group turned me off to the church. The Bible instructs in James 2:2–4, "Suppose a man comes into your meeting wearing a gold ring and fine clothes, and a poor man in shabby clothes also comes in. If you show special attention to the man wearing fine clothes and say, 'Here's a good seat for you,' but say to the poor man, 'You stand there' or 'Sit on the floor by my feet,' have you not discriminated among yourselves and become judges with evil thoughts?" But our leadership openly favored the kids with the designer clothes and money to attend all the expensive ski trips.

There was an accepted "in" clique and those of us who were not part of it did not feel welcome.

On Sunday mornings when I don't want to go to church, I have learned to examine my own soul. Why do I go to church? What am I hoping to gain for myself? What am I willing to give to others and, especially, to God? When I choose to give of myself, God gives me the desire and the energy to honor him and serve others. Then I want to go to church.

The local church did not allow children in the sanctuary. Families were required to place their youngsters in the children's programs. Our family was segregated all week so we asked to sit together but the ushers said we had to comply or leave. I quoted the Scripture, " 'Let the little children come to me, and do not hinder them, for the kingdom of God belongs to such as these. I tell you the truth, anyone who will not receive the kingdom of God like a little child will never enter it.' And he took the children in his arms, put his hands on them and blessed them" (Mark 10:14–16). The response was that children were distracting to adults who wanted to worship. We enjoyed hearing children involved in the worship service and as parents we felt we should decide what was best for our family.

People occasionally told me that they didn't feel welcome or comfortable in my church. Though I never said it to their face, I thought it was always "their" problem. Then I had my tongue pierced. People in my church, including the pastor, treated me coolly and questioned my salvation. Their response hindered my worship time at church. God is easy to deal with but sometimes his people aren't. This experience allowed me to see that our congregation had a problem reaching out and loving people who are "different." I don't have to strive to please man. "Fear of man will prove to be a snare, but whoever trusts in the LORD is kept safe" (Proverbs 29:25). My Father loves me for what's on the inside, and he knows my heart. He knows I'm human, and vulnerable to making mistakes, but he also knows that I love him. Now I look past a person's outward appearance and am better at extending God's love and acceptance to those who are outside the mold.

I was part of a para-church organization that judged a person's spirituality by what version of the Bible he read, whether a woman wore only dresses and head coverings, and the method of child training a family used. This focus on outward appearance and conformance was pursued at the expense of the foundations of biblical faith and Jesus Christ's commands to love one another.

My in-laws have been a strong deterrent to my faith. Involved in an isolationist lifestyle, they have an almost cult-like attitude about not going to church. Living close to them, their relationship to my spouse and me is conditional on us doing what they approve of and they don't approve of my church involvement.

After years in youth group where activities centered on food, fun, and games, I turned eighteen and was no longer welcome with the teenagers. The youth had been segregated from the rest of the church and now I felt betrayed by my peer group. Neither was I prepared to transition from the loud and busy youth group to sitting still for an hour while the pastor delivered a sermon. It broke my parents' hearts when I didn't survive the change, stopped attending church, and acted out my anger with poor lifestyle choices.

Prior to a speaking engagement, the women's pastor oriented me to the weekend's events and the characteristics of the women attending. "Most of the younger women who are married with children work outside the home. They are extremely stressed and we carefully plan several activities on the same weeknight so their families are not being stretched further," she related. "Avoid any nonessential guilt. These ladies have plenty already built in."

As a speaker, this made me soberly consider, "What are the essentials for the family of God?" It is vital that each of us search the Scriptures for ourselves to avoid going beyond what God says. Jesus said, "And you experts in the law, woe to you, because you load people down with burdens they can hardly carry, and you yourselves will not lift one finger to help them" (Luke 11:46).

Taking on burdens the Lord never intended for us to carry results in stress, burnout, and legalism. Our lives must be built on a genuine relationship with God, not on the products a speaker, no matter how good, is promoting.

Mom and Dad threw their creativity and energy into the children's ministries at church. They told everyone

---

how much they loved kids, yet when it was just my folks and me, they didn't have the same exuberance. They gave their best to their ministry projects, but were rather lifeless and distracted for their own children. I resented watching them pour themselves out for other kids while I only got second best from the couple the rest of the church thought was the greatest.

The same week all our community churches were in a lather about the Marilyn Manson concert coming to town, I took my five children to a concert featuring a Christian recording artist at a Christian college. As we took our seats, I was saddened to see all the people who stared disapprovingly at me for bringing children. Paradoxically, Marilyn Manson's concert welcomed all children and provided a lounge room supplied with coffee and donuts for their parents. What a mind-boggling contrast that children were welcomed at an evil place, but not welcome in a Christian setting.

Our pastor and elders were offended if anyone asked questions or suggested doing things a different way.

Questions regarding the pastor's behavior were labeled as gossip. The congregation quickly learned that doubts were bad and that proof of faith was trusting God enough not to question. Conversation did not go beyond the weather and complimenting the pastor. The only acceptable prayer request was for healing for physical illness. Without the freedom to ask questions and have healthy discussions, the church became cold and judgmental toward hurting members. Many people in our church were isolated, wounded, and eventually left the church altogether. If leadership is defensive and not open to a free flow of dialogue, it suffocates a healthy system of checks and balances. Spiritual growth occurs in an environment where people are permitted to ask, and wrestle with, the hard questions of life.

The contradiction between my parents' standards and what was permitted in our youth group was a stumbling block for my faith. While my parents wanted me called by my given name, the youth leader insisted on a nickname. My parents taught that I should save my heart for the time when I was old enough to date, but the youth group encouraged pairing up early. My parents appreciated good manners, while the youth group sponsored activities that centered on being rude and sloppy. At home, I kept my room tidy, but the teens trashed our youth group room twice a week and left the mess for the janitor. Movies shown to the youth group were not good choices. Youth groups are designed to partner with parents to help teens develop a strong faith in God, but the compromising ethics of my youth group created friction between my parents and me.

My adult son and his wife do not attend church though they are both professing Christians. Both served several summers at Christian camp, and both attended church during their courtship, engagement, and first year of marriage. Then they moved to another area and stopped attending church. As their parents, we have encouraged them to get involved in a local congregation, but to no avail. Concern for their spiritual health consumes me. I continue to seek appropriate advice and guidance to pass on to my son and his wife.

A high school friend invited me to church. I knew people dressed up for church so I wore my best skirt. It happened to be a miniskirt, but all my skirts were short. Throughout the morning I was aware of disapproving glances from the women in the church as they viewed my hemline. I knew I was not welcome.

Engaged to a young man in our church, our daughter called off the wedding when he molested her. She also discovered he was involved in pornography. When the incident was brought to the church board's attention, they turned a blind eye on the young man's behavior, but required that our family prove our unconditional forgiveness to the young man by socializing with him and his family. We felt betrayed by the young man who stole our daughter's innocence, and by our church that judged our forgiveness as insufficient and removed our names from membership.

Bible stories did not have an impact on me. What did these once-upon-a-time characters and their obscure problems have to do with me? Then my youth group leader began putting the Bible stories into contemporary settings. Their struggles now looked like the ones I faced in my own life. This method helped me see the relevance of Scripture in my own life and sparked my interest in Bible study and discussion groups where we hammered out biblical principles in everyday life.

As a busy, driven person I have to be accomplishing and producing something all the time. I thrive on being effective and efficient. My childhood church was mired in the ruts of old habits, unchanging leadership, and repetitive themes. It was boring and as soon as I was old enough to make my own decisions, I stopped attending.

In college I followed my heart's conviction that I should return to church and began attending a large congregation that boasted an active college ministry. I surrendered my life to Jesus Christ and began seeking the Lord for myself rather than expecting to be spoon-fed from the pulpit. The first turning point was realizing that not all churches are stodgy. Some move and grow and adapt to changing times and changing audiences. Second, I have a responsibility to God to be an active, contributing part of a healthy fellowship. Church is not a passive activity. Church is a participatory event where I am involved with other believers. It's about me making a sacrifice of time and energy, giving insights and encouragement to other believers.

Church is about reaching out to others with the comfort I have received. It is more about giving than receiving.

A ship in the harbor is safe
But that is not what ships are built for.

—AUTHOR UNKNOWN

Jesus is calling the church to be a community of
wave-riders—people who will lift anchor from what-
ever holds them in life's harbors; people who will sail
off into the high seas of ministry and mission; peo-
ple who will believe that even when God does not
calm the storms, God will calm them in the storms;
people who will know that to voyage with Jesus is to
enjoy peace even in storm-tossed experiences.

—LEONARD SWEET
A Cup of Coffee at the Soul Cafe

A Prodigal's Return

With God, nobody's hopeless.

—RUTH AND BILLY GRAHAM

Every Christian parent watches, prays, and waits for that moment (often at bedtime) when their child begins a conversation about wanting Jesus to come into their heart. There are many variations of this life-changing event. However immature, inexact, or childish the prayer, Mom and Dad trust that this is the seed of eternal life planted in their child's heart.

A Mother's Story (Pat Palau)

Luis and I looked for the affirming signs of spiritual life as our children grew into adolescence. All four of our boys prayed to ask Jesus Christ to be their Savior. Our third son, Andrew, was very friendly and pleasant to be around, but he didn't exhibit a spontaneous, individualized relationship with the Lord.

Like a wise parent, Jesus asked his disciples in Matthew 16:15-17, " 'Who do you say that I am?' Peter quickly responded, 'You are the Christ, the Son of the living God.' Jesus replied, 'Blessed are you, Simon, son of Jonah, for this was not revealed to you by man, but by my Father in heaven.' "

Jesus Christ promised that the church universal would be built not on Peter, but on the overwhelming truth that Simon Peter had articulated—that Jesus Christ was God.

As our son Andrew grew into his teens, there was not a sense of personal identity with Jesus Christ. Faith in God was "our family's thing." Andrew resisted church activities that went beyond fun and games. We are grateful for the patient, overworked youth leaders who hung in there with our beloved son and his group of like-minded pagans!

The following years were marked by Andrew's partying lifestyle, my attempt to corral Andrew into a Christian university, his years in a state college fraternity, and his choice to live a maximum distance from his parents. He worked and lived the life of a worldling. When we were together, Andrew showed respect and was an admirable young man. There just was no light of Jesus in his eyes or his heart. The years went by and he was now twenty-seven years old.

The hound of heaven had not given up on our son. As our ministry prepared to do a series of stadium evangelistic events in Jamaica, we invited Andrew to join us. He came for the sun, beach, and fishing. In Jamaica, Andrew met a godly family; they were deeply involved in the outreach events. As he spent time with their young adult children, he saw a life that was attractive. God spoke to his heart in a powerful way. In the presence of his new Christian friends, our prodigal repented of his years of wandering.

The local church is part of God's plan for birth, care, feeding, and restoration of our children. How thankful I am for those mature men and women who taught and mentored our children through their rebellious or awkward years. Remaining in one church all these years meant that our children, for vice or virtue, were well known.

As missionaries commissioned and sent out by our church, I winced at how closely our family was observed. I decided early on that I would rather be seen as the less than perfect tribe we were than be isolated without others to come alongside and pray for us. It is risky to be known. Being known means I am the possible topic of gossip. Being known also means I am the recipient of support from mature believers who care and bring my family before the Father in prayer.

A year after his return to Jesus Christ, Andrew came back to our home church. Standing before the congregation, he told them what God had done and thanked the long-suffering church for loving him, accepting him, and faithfully praying him into an authentic relationship with Christ.

Several of Andrew's Sunday school teachers have since told me funny and maddening stories of Andrew and his friends in their youth group, Sunday school classes, and Boys' Brigade. These faithful mentors put up with Andrew's shenanigans and never stopped praying for him. Nor did they gossip—though they had plenty of material. Today they take deserved pride in what God is doing through Andrew's life.

Relating to irregular and difficult children is a challenge that demands maturity and wisdom beyond human skills. Those of us serving in local churches are amateurs with the Holy Spirit at our side. The Andrews of this world keep us going.

Because I have such a deep love for the church's prodigals, I have observed what does and doesn't help them.

- Reacting every time a child complains about church is not helpful. "If we went to such and such church, I'd go without whining." Maybe yes, and maybe no. I once spoke to a youth leader about my child's complaint only to have him say, "Your son is not here often enough to be aware of what our program includes."

- Church leaders must decide whether to blend in to the church family, hide out, or sit on the fringes to protect their children. People brought me tales about my child's antics. Sometimes they were indulging in gossip concerning leadership children, secretly gloating in the fact that these kids were not perfect. That these truths involved my children magnified my pain. I didn't want my children to endure unfair scrutiny, or be held to a higher standard than others. It was tempting to withdraw and not let anyone close. Yet beneath the emotion of the encounter and the possible motives of the messenger, there was an element of truth that needed to be faced. It was important that I didn't "shoot the messenger."
- The people who expressed genuine concern, and spoke the truth in love, supported the ministry by caring for our family. They prayed us through hard times.
- When Luis and I were struggling with behavioral issues with Andrew, we read John White's book, *Parents in Pain* (IVP, 1979). I also found comfort

in Ruth Bell Graham's poems about prodigals as well as her written experiences with her own prodigal son.

Ultimately in God's mercy, Andrew married his beautiful wife, Wendy, whom he met in Jamaica. With two sons of their own, today Andrew and Wendy serve the Lord wholeheartedly. Andrew works in evangelism, sharing his testimony, reaching those who have wandered away from the faith, or were never truly born into the family of God. He has been instrumental in developing a unique model of evangelism and directing events nationwide that attract hundreds of thousands of people who come to hear the Gospel.

The vision of every Sunday school worker and parent of a prodigal is that God will harness the wanderer's creativity, feistiness, and restlessness to the power of the Holy Spirit to turn the world upside down. Andrew believes people should never give up faithfully praying for, and inviting family and friends to know Jesus Christ.

Not long ago, our family experienced one of the great events of our lives. We hosted a two-day evangelistic festival in our hometown of Portland, Oregon. About 140,000 people attended the festival that included hours of contemporary music and several Gospel presentations by Luis. Many of these evangelistic ideas originated with Andrew, who freshly remembers how unbelievers think. We all worked on this: Luis and me, our sons, our daughters-in-law. To be a whole family in ministry to reach the lost is the best dream come true.

Too many teens and adults raised in the church have wandered from the faith or defy it outright. Sometimes a lack of conflict lulls parents into complacency until the drugs, alcohol, or birth control pills are discovered. Serial killer Ted Bundy and occult rock star Marilyn Manson were reportedly raised in Christian homes. According to *New Man* magazine, Manson was ordained in the First Church of Satan. Is there any rhyme or reason to why some children stray and others hold fast to Jesus Christ? Parents often ask, "Where did I go wrong?"

Not all prodigals march resolutely off into the world, leaving family, church, and lifestyle behind. In fact, these brave types are the minority. Condoleeza Rice was no rebel, but she has called herself a onetime prodigal. A preacher's kid, she grew up in church but drifted from her faith in her mid-twenties. Ups and downs in her faith, coupled with work, studies, and international travel interfered with regular church attendance. During a rare visit to church, a sermon about the Prodigal Son's older brother sparked her return to active participation in the local church. Immediately upon moving into the White House as President George W. Bush's National Security advisor, she chose a church, committed herself to it, and took membership classes. Knowing the pressures she would face, this was a wise decision.

Leaving church is not usually a dramatic departure, just a slow drift.

> *"Jesus was a daring bridge builder. Against his own overwhelming odds, he imagined a bridge of unprecedented spiritual influence—one that could span a chasm roaring with skepticism, indifference, hostility, even persecution. He imagined a bridge able to connect his people—"my church," He called them—to a believing, disinterested world. That's why Jesus loved to talk about the church, especially the power it could unleash and exercise in the world. This is the bridge Jesus imagined: a connecting church—a bridge of influence. We can no longer simply afford to stand on one side of the Great Chasm and shout to those on the other side. We must connect."*
>
> — ROBERT LEWIS
> *The Church of Irresistible Influence*

What Others Say about Church

My exit from the church came not with a big bang, but as a slow leak. In my late teens and early college years it was hard to find a church that felt like home. I stayed up late Saturday nights and then excused myself from meeting with my brothers and sisters in Christ to celebrate the Lord's Day. Interestingly, this slow drift from my spiritual family during my college studies was socially acceptable, much like the workaholic who is excused from making time to be with his physical family. Returning home for Christmas, my family's steadfastness in their faith commitment showed me how far I had roamed and caused me to think, "I haven't been to church in years. I don't pray. I call myself a Christian, yet I've allowed life to carry me along without making a decision to choose a church and join it." After the holiday break, I plugged into my college Christian community.

After a humiliating divorce, it was too painful to return to church. My change in status was embarrassing and I felt judged by the church that I wasn't spiritual enough to make the marriage work. I experienced a "spiritual crack-up." Drowning in deep emotional pain, I stopped going to church, which should have been the best hospital in the world for me.

Through the two disciplines of daily Bible reading and prayer, the Lord gently showed me that he is steady and worthy of my trust. His church consists of people who are not perfect. Eventually I was able to turn my eyes on Jesus and take them off people.

Feeling drawn back to fellowship, I found a new church home where I felt safe and understood, challenged and loved. This church understood my peculiar needs as a divorced person. I recommitted my life to Jesus Christ in a specific surrender.

I often think of how frighteningly easy it was to resign from the corporate church. I had a close call.

Two of our twenty-something-year-old sons have chosen to experiment with drugs and be sexually active with their non-Christian girlfriends. Needless to say, their choices have drawn them far away from their walk with God. While we are deeply disappointed with the direction they've chosen, we believe that their journeys are their own with God. He, not us, will teach them, guide them, and ultimately bring them back into fellowship with himself. Our job is to love them unconditionally as God does, to look past their lifestyles, and to appreciate them as adults. And to pray, pray, pray.

Pursuing my career, I drifted from my Christian faith and rarely attended Sunday worship. On a sporadic visit to church, I saw myself like the older brother of the Prodigal Son who was self-satisfied and complacent in faith. Like the older brother, I never doubted the existence of God, but I wasn't actively walking in faith either. Recommitting my life to Jesus Christ, I embarked on an active prayer life, began Bible study, and got involved regularly in church. It was an important turning point.

I was raised in a Christian home but not solidly grounded in my faith. At nineteen years of age I took a college course in comparative religions. That course was enough to steer me away from my childhood moorings. Though I was convinced there was a God, I was not convinced there was a Jesus. One cannot come to God except through Jesus. I walked away from my family, turned to alcohol, and became suicidal. Successful in academics and in my job, I had a problem with arrogance. I thought I had come to a reasoned conclusion about my faith, yet what I remember most was unrelenting sadness.

A friend invited me to a Bible study that I attended off and on for a couple of years. My friend was a smart woman and I enjoyed our intellectual discussions about faith. She told me about Jesus Christ and I tried to talk her out of her beliefs. She invited me to a seminar on hermeneutics where the speaker said I must be born again to understand the Bible. He told me to go home and settle my issues with Jesus. It was the love of Jesus that overmastered me. I invited the Lord into my heart then went to sleep.

In the morning I could feel that Christ was in my heart. He had made a difference: "it took." The Lord brought unrelenting joy into my heart and the change was so visibly evident that when I saw my friend, she exclaimed, "You did it!" My life turned around one hundred and eighty degrees. I was a terrific pagan; now I am fervent for the Lord. Though life is often hard, I know Jesus Christ is with me, he loves me, and gives me his joy.

My parents were both seminary graduates and worked in full-time ministry positions. Though they may have been tempted to feel "above" the local church and criticize the imperfections of our congregation, they never did. Their respect for the church was evident every Sunday as our family attended church and Sunday school. They were not casual about church involvement, nor did they view attendance as optional. That example during my childhood drew me back to the church when I was grown. I knew the church was the place to go in time of crisis. Their attitude toward the church paved the way for me to come back when I needed a local congregation as an adult.

I grew up in church but quit attending at age fifteen when my dad died of cancer. At twenty-seven, some friends invited me to their congregation. The pastor and people befriended me. They were real folks who offered me their friendship and introduced me to a relationship with the best friend of all, Jesus Christ.

As a child I went to Sunday school, but once I achieved moderate success in college and in my career, I had little need for God. I was able to handle life on my own. Then a crisis came that I was not able to deal with. That's when I realized I needed a Savior, someone who was greater than me. I sought God on my knees and found a church filled with others who knew they needed the Lord.

Though my dad was the pastor of the Holiness church I grew up in, I ran from the Lord. I was middle-aged and cynical when my third wife encouraged me to visit my sister and brother-in-law, who are Christians. My hostility toward Christianity had caused me to be estranged from them. My sister and her husband were gracious and welcoming. If they had preached at me I would have walked out. Instead, their genuine interest in me attracted me back into relationship with them and I went to church where I gave my heart to the Lord.

After ten years away from the church, I rekindled an old childhood friendship. My friend had steadfastly held to Christian principles while I had exchanged God's plan for the world's philosophies. By drifting from the church, I did not have the standard of the Word proclaimed weekly to keep me anchored when I made serious life-changing commitments, including marriage. Without preaching, my friend's gentle conversations with me quickly reminded me that I had moved far from the Christian mind-set of my past. The assurance that there are absolute truths and godly principles that I could count on drew me back to the Lord like a moth to a light.

As an adolescent, I was not clearly labeled a rebel. I merely wanted to swim in both ponds. I wanted to live like my friends, tiptoe around the edge of the pond with risky behaviors, and disregard God. Yet, I also liked the family pond with their focus on Christ and the church as our place of connection.

Disliking confrontation, I was "big man on campus" and still attended church where I arrived late and left early. My heart wasn't in it. I felt sad when I deceived my parents regarding my whereabouts and activities. I never felt rejected or less loved by my family, nor did I feel that the youth leaders were looking over my shoulder.

Then in my midtwenties I gave my life wholeheartedly to the Lord. Looking back, neither my parents nor ministry leaders could have changed things. My decisions were under my control. There was not some theological or practical issue of the Christian faith that tripped me up. I knew and chose my path deliberately.

Reading the biblical account of the Prodigal Son, I see myself some days as the prodigal, some days as the elder brother, and some days as the father.

I was a child when my parents divorced. Our denomination viewed divorce as the unforgivable sin and people shunned my mother and me. This rejection caused my mother to stop attending church.

As an adolescent, I walked to Sunday school. Walking home alone in the rain while those from my church drove past me, I felt unwanted by the congregation and finally stopped attending. Though I continued the disciplines of daily prayer and Bible reading, I was adrift spiritually. I tried going to other churches during my high school and college years, but each attempt was disastrous.

Married and expecting my first child, the Lord stirred my spirit. I wanted my baby to grow up in a church family and to know the Bible stories. I suggested church to my husband and he agreed. The Lord literally drew me back to himself.

Every saint has a past and every sinner has a future.

—AL EGG, CHAPLAIN,
Portland Trailblazers Basketball Team

A Father's Story (Luis Palau)

The moments immediately before I stand to preach the Gospel of Jesus Christ to a crowd of thousands hold a wild mixture of emotions.

There's thankfulness to God for granting me another harvest time opportunity. There's anticipation and joy, knowing that God is patiently at work in many hearts, "not wanting anyone to perish, but everyone to come to repentance" (2 Peter 3:9). And for many years, there was sadness because the thoughts of this father would almost always turn to Andrew.

Andrew is the third of my four sons. After graduating from college, Andrew moved to Boston where, as a confident young man, he began his climb up the corporate ladder. But it wasn't his distance from home that troubled my heart; it was his distance from the Lord.

Like our other sons, Andrew had prayed to invite Jesus to come into his heart when he was a child. Since high school, however, he had little interest in the Bible and church. Fraternity life ruled in college, where Andrew followed the path of least resistance. God occasionally stepped in, but could not fit in. Now living on the other side of the continent, Andrew lived a secular lifestyle with secular values.

Painful as it was, Pat and I had to accept what we had counseled other parents. Just because Andrew was brought up in Sunday school and could talk the language did not mean he was truly converted. Conversion is essential for everyone, whether born into a pagan family or a totally absorbing Christian family.

So it was that, as I sat on the platform and prayed, "Lord, may many come forward to confess Christ," at that moment I'd be thinking, "*There's no greater joy than this . . . but how can my joy be complete until Andrew stands here as one who walks with Christ?*"

An element of sadness permeated my life. I realized that, if my heart carried this weight, God's heart is even more saddened because his love is so much more self-less and pure. This truth is at the heart of Jesus' assertion in the Sermon on the Mount: "If you, then, though you are evil, know how to give good gifts to your children, how much more will your Father in heaven give good gifts to those who ask him!" (Matthew 7:11).

Andrew's rebellion was a painful lesson. Because one of my sons, whom I did my very best to channel in the ways of Christ, resisted conversion, I was kept from certain aspects of arrogance and from self-right-eousness. I was not so charming and wonderful as to cause Andrew to walk as a saint and never besmirch the name of Christ.

I could do no more than cling to God's promise to Israel: "All your sons will be taught by the LORD, and great will be your children's peace" (Isaiah 54:13).

In 1992, all glory to God, Andrew returned to the Lord. Was it a first-time repentance and genuine belief? To me it doesn't matter if I know exactly when my son was converted—as a child or at age twenty-seven. My joy is that Andrew is born of God and bearing the fruit of biblical sonship.

I now preach the Gospel with even more conviction. The resurrected Lord Jesus Christ has power to change America, where eighty percent claim to be Christians, but relatively few live any differently from pagans or atheists. Their hearts have not been changed, and unless Jesus Christ changes their hearts, they never will be any different from those outside the Christian faith.

To me, Andrew is a beautiful picture of what I'd like to see God do for the children and youth of America.

There was a man who had two sons. The younger one said to his father, "Father, give me my share of the estate." So he divided his property between them. Not long after that, the younger son got together all he had, set off for a distant country and there squandered his wealth in wild living. After he had spent everything, there was a severe famine in that whole country, and he began to be in need. So he went and hired himself out to a citizen of that country, who sent him to his fields to feed pigs. He longed to fill his stomach with the pods that the pigs were eating, but no one gave him anything.

When he came to his senses, he said, "How many of my father's hired men have food to spare, and here I am starving to death! I will set out and go back to my father and say to him: Father, I have sinned against heaven and against you. I am no longer worthy to be called your son; make me like one of your hired men." So he got up and went to his father.

But while he was still a long way off, his father saw him and was filled with compassion for him; he ran to his son, threw his arms around him and kissed him. The son said to him, "Father, I have sinned against heaven and against you. I am no longer worthy to be called your son."

But the father said to his servants, "Quick! Bring the best robe and put it on him. Put a ring on his finger and sandals on his feet. Bring the fattened calf and kill it. Let's have a feast and celebrate. For this son of mine was dead and is alive again; he was lost and is found. So they began to celebrate.

—LUKE 15:11–24

A Church to Grow In

I rejoiced with those who said to me,
"Let us go to the house of the LORD."

—PSALM 122:1

Christians who did not grow up in Christian homes know the overpowering conversion experience of discovering Jesus Christ. Becoming believers as adults, these people personally understand the difference between a life with God and a life without God. They live every day knowing the difference, overwhelmed that God loved them enough to rescue them.

Our creative God is constantly reaching out and drawing people to himself. "But I, when I am lifted up from the earth, will draw all men to myself" (John 12:32).

The Lord's creativity is endless as he invites us into a personal relationship with him through mentors, evangelistic campaigns, festivals, films, concerts, radio, television, literature, vacation Bible schools, Christian camps, Christian schools, rescue missions, Bible studies, campus ministries, prison ministries, and other para-church organizations that reach out to professionals.

Once someone prays a simple prayer asking Jesus Christ to be his Lord and Savior (and, thankfully, becoming a Christian is indeed simple), that newborn Christian suddenly has innumerable brothers and sisters in Christ.

No matter how chronologically old the new Christian is, he is a newborn to the things of God. Most evangelism takes place away from the church in neutral venues where unbelievers feel comfortable. After an evangelistic evening of fabulous contemporary music followed by a presentation of the Good News about Jesus Christ, what a glorious sight to see individuals come forward and give their hearts to the Savior. The "baby" Christian needs to quickly find a church home where he can be nurtured, and taught to grow in the faith.

If you helped introduce someone to Jesus Christ, also help that new Christian settle into a solidly biblical church. If you are a new believer, go to church with the friend who brought you to hear the Gospel. Attend a church in your neighborhood or one where you have some past connection. Look in the newspaper and telephone book for a church that offers appropriate programs for your age and needs. Find a church that preaches and teaches the same message you heard when you gave your life to Jesus Christ. The church must teach from the Bible as the authoritative Word of God, and hold Christ as the center of worship.

Everyone has a unique conversion story. What an amazing God who honors our individuality! Even though there is only one way to salvation—through Jesus Christ—God reaches each person's heart in a different way.

> *That if you confess with your mouth, "Jesus is Lord," and believe in your heart that God raised him from the dead, you will be saved. For it is with your heart that you believe and are justified, and it is with your mouth that you confess and are saved.*
>
> —ROMANS 10:9, 10

What Others Say about Church

A woman who attended the church where I grew up prayed for me while I was away in the military service. At age forty-one I returned to the church and accepted Christ as my Lord and Savior. She approached me after service and said, "Now I can stop praying."

As a rebellious teenager attending Marilyn Manson concerts, I used to make fun of Christians. Thinking that we are all good in our own way, I didn't believe God would send anyone to hell. Acceptance and tolerance were my clarion call. At work, a Christian man asked what I believed and listened without interrupting. He kept inviting me to attend church until I went. I wept through the service; I wanted what those believers had. At a Ray Boltz concert, the video showing Christ carrying the cross to Calvary for me propelled me to go forward and ask Jesus into my heart. Later, I led my parents and siblings to the Lord and I married that Christian man I worked with.

An outdoor festival came to our town one summer. There had been plenty of publicity, so I went to check out this big outdoor party. For two evenings, people picnicked on blankets and listened to hours of music. Artists painted faces while explaining the Gospel with their colors and there were areas for kids to watch *Veggie Tales* and *Bibleman* videos. People with all kinds of unique talents like skateboarding gave demonstrations and shared their testimonies. The atmosphere was welcoming and festive as Luis Palau spoke simply about Jesus Christ.

Though I would not darken a church door, the festival brought the church to me. Seeing Christians have fun, share their resources with the community, and bring the Gospel to the streets with no strings attached changed my stereotyped image of Christians. I wanted to be a part of that party. I gave my heart to Jesus that summer. I'm looking forward to the eternal party we will share with Jesus Christ.

An acquaintance invited me to attend a drama of the Last Supper at his church. The production was spectacular and I went home hungry to know more about that event and the disciples who had been part of it. For months I read through the Gospels, focusing on the last half of Matthew, Mark, Luke, and John to discover more about Jesus and the lives of his followers. Then my friend invited me to attend his church's dramatic depiction of the life of Jesus Christ. Watching what Christ endured on the cross on my behalf made it an easy step to give my heart to the Lord. Now as a member of the drama team, I know how much work and time go into such an event. I'm thankful for those who gave their talents to "show" me Jesus.

Neighbors invited me to Vacation Bible School at their church. I was too bashful to go forward during the altar call, but I went home, knelt by my bed, and invited Jesus to be my Lord and Savior.

My friend was a seriously ill diabetic who prayed for me. I had tried sex, drugs—everything except the Lord—to fill my unhappiness. In a desperate situation, I decided to kill myself. Then I turned on the radio where a pastor introduced me to a true friend. I prayed and asked God to be my forever friend.

The next day, I asked God what I should do about the apartment I had arranged to rent with my lover. The Holy Spirit impressed on me to send the key back. Though I lost the first month's rent, it was a small price to be free of the situation. How wonderful to have a Savior who cared to answer my questions and guide me. I telephoned my praying friend to tell her of my decision. She rejoiced and said she could die now that I had come into the kingdom. Six months later she passed away, but not before she prayed me into eternity.

Living outside the United States, our family attended a church for English-speaking expatriates. My children went to a Sunday school class taught by a sweet, young Wycliffe missionary. Each week that teacher faithfully proclaimed the Gospel over and over to wiggly young students. Sunday after Sunday, my children asked Jesus into their hearts. Certainly Jesus does not come and go, so I reassured my children that Jesus heard them the first time and that he would never leave. Repeating a prayer on a weekly basis may not have been doctrinally correct, yet today my children are grown with youngsters of their own and they date their conversion experience back to that Sunday school class. 1 Corinthians 13:11 says, "When I was a child, I talked like a child, I thought like a child, I reasoned like a child. When I became a man, I put childish ways behind me." God sorts out the details, considers our childish thinking and leads us to maturity.

As adolescents, my cousins began attending a local church because the pastor was good looking, and they invited me to come along. Though they eventually drifted away, I continued to attend. The pastor preached a "hellfire and brimstone" style sermon and I accepted Jesus Christ as my Lord and Savior. That was thirty years ago and I still have an appreciation for that style of preaching.

I was raised in a home that mixed aspects of Christianity with witchcraft. My public school allowed all religions except Christianity to present their beliefs. By age thirty I was entrenched in the world system and my life was falling apart. Two husbands had left me for other women, I hated myself, and I decided it would be less of a burden to my children if I killed myself. My plan was to leave huge bills that my ex-husband would have to pay for the rest of his life. The morning I was to carry out my plan, a voice in my heart said, "You've tried everything but church. When you kill yourself and stand before God and he asks why you didn't try church, what will you say?" That Sunday the pastor's message said my messed up life could have a second chance. The woman sitting next to me turned and said she would go with me to the front of the church. I didn't have to go alone. That was twenty years ago.

Attending a Christian college cemented my faith. Staying up late at night with other students (and occasionally faculty members) to talk and hash over beliefs and principles caused me to seriously take stock of what I believed.

The only child of devoted, loving parents, my upbringing was remarkably secure and stable. My parents made countless sacrifices to provide me with every educational opportunity. Though I was pampered, my parents held high moral standards and expectations for me. With their example of integrity, they taught me about fairness, right from wrong, and the benefits of discipline and hard work. A perfect childhood; yet something was missing. No matter how hard I worked, I could never be perfect.

Other children in my neighborhood and at school were different. They had something I didn't have. This difference was Jesus. Occasionally friends took me to evangelistic outreaches but, being a shy person, I found the altar calls terrifying. Other teens argued with me about spiritual matters and told me I was going to hell. That approach alienated me as I asked questions and explored Christianity. The friends who made a lasting impact on me were those who developed a friendship with me and loved me like Jesus would. They performed unselfish acts of kindness for others, expecting nothing in return. I could not argue with their example.

After many years of searching, I became a Christian at a college Bible study. Because of my parents' deep love for me, I easily understood that God was my faithful, loving Father. Some of my adult friends who endured abusive fathers or were abandoned by their dads struggle with this truth. Because I did not grow up in the church, every discovery about biblical truth was fresh and exciting, unfettered by baggage. Some of my adult friends who grew up in the church could not reconcile the hypocrisy they daily observed with Sunday morning Christianity, and they walked away from God.

Today, my greatest joy comes from watching my own teenagers rub shoulders with fellow school students, leading them to Jesus Christ through their example and friendship. My husband also became a Christian later in life, so we purposefully did not homeschool our children or put them in Christian school. Young people are the most effective evangelizers of other young people, and their faith is strengthened and refined through the process.

While I was in beauty school, one customer always asked for me. A lovely Christian woman, she embodied what I wanted to be. She often brought me pretty gifts and prayer cards. When I took a job at a Christian business, my coworkers encouraged me to go to church. At the church's women's retreat I accepted Jesus as my Lord and Savior. When I returned home from the retreat, my husband met me with a box he had found in the attic. I recognized it as one of the gifts from that gracious lady so many years ago. I opened the package and inside were homemade placemats she had given me for when I was married. God spoke to me in that moment—he had sent someone to me ten years ago and had been patiently waiting for me ever since.

Flying home from a business trip, the man seated next to me began polite conversation. I told him I had recently been diagnosed with bone cancer. The man explained that he had watched his own father die at age thirty-four. His father's peaceful example had encouraged this man to seek Jesus Christ as his own Lord and Savior, and now he wondered if I had the same peace. He explained the plan of salvation and introduced me to Jesus Christ.

Growing up in a traditional Protestant church, I learned about God, but to the exclusion of a personal relationship with Jesus Christ. When I was nineteen years old, a young woman at a secular summer camp told me the truth about Jesus. Although I believed in God and knew that "Jesus died for my sins," I thought God was purely interested in my good works and achievements. Those things were the pathways to love in my family, which was horribly imbalanced by my father's alcoholism. I had no frame of reference for the healthy, fatherly love about which my friend spoke. Desperate for the unconditional love of Jesus Christ, it was easy to understand my need for forgiveness, but hard to accept that God wanted to give me a new start.

After wrestling with this new information for two weeks, I got down on my knees in the living room when no one else was at home and prayed, "Jesus, if you are real, please come into my heart and change my life. I can't go on like this." It's hard to describe the tremendous sense of peace that came over me in that moment. An inaudible voice told me, "You are going to be okay." The joy that stirred my heart on that day ushered me onto a path of following Jesus Christ throughout college and beyond. Now, whenever I have the chance, I take great joy in telling others about this amazing, restoring love.

I was raised in a nonreligious, evolutionist home. I assumed everyone was an evolutionist because it was taught as fact in school. When a girl tried to witness to me shortly after I got to college, I pointed to the "tree of life" in an evolutionary book and told her, "This is my bible." A few times I attempted to reconcile evolution with Genesis but decided to leave that to the theological experts. When I heard a radio program about creationism, it dawned on me that I didn't have to believe in evolution when creation fit the available evidence better. I sent for literature and tapes, and attended seminars and conferences featuring creationist speakers. These teachings proved that the Bible is completely trustworthy from the very first verse and that Jesus is the Creator and Savior.

Though we raised our children in the church, my daughter's faith caught on fire when she attended camps, conferences, and services outside of our church. I am thankful for Christian ministries that sponsor outreach programs beyond their own church, and provide opportunities for people to meet Jesus Christ and to grow in their faith.

For God did not send his Son into the world to condemn the world, but to save the world through him.

—JOHN 3:17

The Church and Its Habits

*So Joshua called together the twelve men he had
appointed from the Israelites, one from each tribe,
and said to them, "Go over before the ark of the
LORD your God into the middle of the Jordan.
Each of you is to take up a stone on his shoulder,
according to the number of the tribes of the Israelites,
to serve as a sign among you. In the future, when
your children ask you, "What do these stones
mean?" tell them that the flow of the Jordan was
cut off before the Ark of the Covenant of the LORD.
When it crossed the Jordan, the waters of the Jordan
were cut off. These stones are to be a memorial to the
people of Israel forever."*

—JOSHUA 4:4–7

Spiritual traditions are important. Scripture is filled with spiritual traditions that the Lord instructed his people to keep.

In the Old Testament, life had a rhythm for the children of Israel. They enjoyed a seventh day of rest, festivals, and celebrations throughout the year to remind the people of God's gracious interventions in their history. Spiritual traditions were vital because, like us, the Israelites quickly drifted into the patterns of the people who lived around them.

In the New Testament, gathering together for worship, fellowship, prayer, and praise are mentioned in the text as a foregone conclusion. It was natural—a felt need. In early church history, Sunday was the chosen day to remember and celebrate Jesus Christ's resurrection. It is a spiritual tradition we continue today.

When my children were small, they wore high-topped white shoes. Saturday night, in preparation for church, I polished their shoes and laid them out with the clothes they were going to wear. A great deal of the success and blessings of the Sunday morning experience comes because of what happens the night before. Because all families are different in every way, a good question to answer in a calm, quiet moment is, "What can I do to make the preparation for church a reasonably pleasant experience?" This may seem unspiritual, but remember: it is a fallen world and things do get mislaid and orange juice does get spilled.

One friend gets her four lively children up an hour earlier than necessary for a Sunday breakfast of waffles, bacon, and eggs. She says this is something not manageable on busy school days, though I don't know how she manages it on Sundays. She wants Sunday memories to be special.

My one great fear as I write this is that some will see it as one more burden added on to an already stressful life. You have to differentiate between options, suggestions, and biblical commands. Most of us do this poorly. The overburdened suck up every suggestion with no regard for their unique situation. A suggestion is just that—a possibility, an option.

The Gospels described the Pharisees as people who, "tie up heavy loads and put them on men's shoulders, but they themselves are not willing to lift a finger to move them" (Matthew 23:4). Cold cereal, cinnamon rolls, or bagels may be a more convenient Sunday breakfast for your family. Please use these ideas as suggestions—use what works for your family. But if any of these suggestions help your family prepare for and enjoy Sunday mornings, I'll be delighted.

After making the world in six days, our Creator was pleased with what he had done and he rested. "Six days you shall labor and do all your work, but the seventh day is a Sabbath to the LORD your God," instructs Deuteronomy 5:13, 14. The balance between rest and work is lived by faith. The benefits and rewards are seen in the long term. Those six days of hard, focused work are validated and productive because of the one day of total change of pace, rest, and worship.

We ought to try it. Perhaps our burn out and fatigue are the result of working like insane people and then crashing for the two weeks each year that we call vacation. God prescribed a balanced program of labor and rest that included one day each week of Sabbath rest. Americans typically work very hard. Other Western societies enjoy much more holiday rest breaks in their annual schedules. A good place to begin is to incorporate the spiritual tradition of honoring the Sabbath. This doesn't mean becoming legalistic about the Jewish laws of doing no work on Saturday. It means taking time out to rest our bodies and souls as we worship God.

The New Testament outlines three spiritual traditions for the church. First, believers meet together regularly. Second, believers remember the Lord's death on our behalf through the practice of communion. Third, believers participate in baptism, identifying us with Jesus Christ and his people. We have added our own customs and spiritual traditions that keep us focused on our relationship with the Lord Jesus Christ.

But as for me and my household, we will serve the LORD.

—JOSHUA 24:15

What Others Say about Church

As soon as each of us children could read, Mama started us on our own "Bible Diary." Beginning with the two most story-like books of the Bible, *Ruth* and *Esther,* she instructed us to read one chapter from the Bible each day. In my diary, I then recorded the date, the chapter read, and wrote a one-sentence summary of that chapter. Next, I wrote a word from the chapter that I did not understand along with its meaning copied from the dictionary. Last, I copied a favorite verse from the chapter into the notebook. This became my morning practice. When the notebook was filled, a new notebook was begun. Today I still return to the practice of the Bible diary in between other Bible studies. My collection of notebooks begun when I was six years old is a testimony of my growth in study of the Scripture and my relationship with the Lord.

Sunday afternoons at our house meant a special meal together. Mother planned ahead and put something to slow bake in the oven or in the Crock-Pot before we left for church. I have fond memories of returning home after worship each week to the welcoming smells of sumptuous meals. It was wonderful to sit down together around the table, often with friends, but always without the week's appointments that pulled us apart.

As a college student I recall many Sundays being very close to asleep during the church service because I had been so late to bed the night before. Now it is tradition to get my family and myself to bed in a timely fashion on Saturday night.

In our family we memorized the books of the Bible when we were five years old so we could easily find our way around the Bible. Mom recited five books in sequence each day until I could repeat them back. Then the next five books were added to the repetition. Once I could recite all sixty-six books in order, all the family gathered for the presentation. The prize for memorizing the books of the Bible was a real Bible all my own from my parents.

After dinner and baths, all eight of us pajama-clad children gathered in the living room while Mom or Dad read the Bible for a half hour. Frequently someone had a question that sparked interesting conversations about applying Scripture to our daily lives. As one of the youngest children, it was not uncommon for me to fall asleep while one of my parents was reading. It was a cozy feeling to drift to sleep surrounded by my family and in the presence of the Lord.

Our church hired an associate pastor to join the staff. Once the decision was official, members of the congregation began corresponding with the associate pastor and his wife during the months it took them to relocate to our state. Reminiscent of a courtship, our letters and e-mails back and forth helped everyone get to know one another. Arriving in town, the associate pastor and his wife found a basket in their new home filled with gift certificates to the local hardware store, newspaper, garbage service, and restaurants. A map accompanied coupons to area attractions. A phone card was included with a note to keep in touch with friends from their previous city, and several phone numbers for church members were listed with an invitation to "use them often." Successful as a tangible welcome gift, the basket has become a standard way of welcoming new people into our church family.

Depending on Dad's work schedule, sometimes we gathered for family devotions in the morning, sometimes at lunch, most times just before bed. Dad read a chapter from the Old Testament, one from Psalms, one from Proverbs, and one from the New Testament. Then we rehearsed Scripture we had previously memorized and practiced the current verses we were working on. From preschooler to Mom and Dad, one verse at a time, together we memorized classic passages like the Ten Commandments, John 1, Luke 2 and Matthew 2, 1 Corinthians 13, Psalm 23, Psalm 100, and others. We sang songs together, mostly children's Bible songs for the little children, and prayed aloud beginning with the youngest and continuing to the oldest. My favorite part was at the end when Dad prayed a blessing over us from Scriptures, such as Numbers 6:24–26, Psalm 28, Ephesians 3:14–21, and Hebrews 12:1–3. These times made the Bible a familiar and fun part of daily family life.

When she was a teenager, my mother sometimes struggled with thinking her faith was not real because she had trusted Jesus Christ at such an early age. When each of us four children trusted in Christ, Mother treated our spiritual "birthday" as a huge event. She videotaped each child telling his story. The annual celebration of our spiritual birthdays includes cake, decorations, and watching the video.

Each week Dad took one of us to breakfast at the only restaurant in town, the local greasy spoon diner. The waitress knew us so well that she brought Dad a cup of coffee and me a hot chocolate every time without asking. During our morning conversation, Dad asked four questions: How are you doing? How is your relationship with the other family members? How are you doing with your studies and your goals and dreams? How is your relationship with the Lord? I treasured my dates with Dad. These days I am taking my own children on breakfast dates. I still talk weekly with Dad and he still asks the same questions that keep me on track in my Christian walk.

I am on the mailing list to receive occasional letters from a missionary whom I consider a spiritual mentor. I cut out parts of these letters and use them for bookmarks in my Bible so I can remember and meditate on these encouraging words.

"Taste and see that the LORD is good" (Psalm 34:8) was my parents' motto. Each evening our family enjoyed dessert while Dad read the Bible aloud. As each child learned to read, the Bible was passed around the table and we all read a couple of verses before passing the chapter to the next person to continue reading. Everyone felt important to the process of reading the Word of God aloud daily.

Due to Dad's career in professional sports, Easter was a nonexistent holiday as everyone was moving or traveling that week. Mom began a tradition called "Road to Calvary." Each day during the week immediately proceeding Easter, we read the Bible chapters depicting Jesus

Christ's last week before the crucifixion. Easter morning we would race to each other to proclaim, "He is risen!" and receive the enthusiastic response, "He is risen indeed!" Mom made a colorful banner for the occasion that read, "He Is Risen," and hung it up each year on Easter morning. Our Easter celebration affirmed the importance of the resurrection to our faith no matter where we were or what else was going on in our lives.

As a young mother, Sunday mornings were anything but calm as my husband and I dashed around getting our baby and us out the door on time for church. Time and again we found ourselves piled into the station wagon in an unworshipful state. Frustrated, I recalled my own childhood and how my parents managed to make Sundays pleasant. Saturday night, my mother made sure everyone was bathed and their Sunday clothes, including shoes, were set out for the next morning. As the head of the household, my dad exemplified that church was important by being the first to rise on Sunday morning and wake the rest of us in plenty of time to get ready. By adopting the Sunday traditions my parents had used, my husband and I have made Sunday pleasant for our family.

My parents took seriously the part about Sunday being a day of rest. Afternoons were spent playing table games inside, or baseball outside. Our family read books aloud and took walks to feed the ducks and enjoy God's creation.

When I was a child, churches held regular Sunday evening services featuring training classes, prayer sessions, reports from returning missionaries, vesper services, or traveling Gospel singing groups. The evening services were casual and fun. Today, Sunday evening services are nearly a thing of the past but our family uses that time for fun get-togethers with friends and newcomers.

> *And he took bread, gave thanks and broke it, and gave it to them, saying, "This is my body given for you; do this in remembrance of me."*
>
> —LUKE 22:19

SECTION III

The Church as a
Dysfunctional Family

The Church and Its Conflicts

The eye cannot say to the hand, "I don't need you!" And the head cannot say to the feet, "I don't need you!" On the contrary, those parts of the body that seem to be weaker are indispensable, and the parts that we think are less honorable we treat with special honor. And the parts that are unpresentable are treated with special modesty, while our presentable parts need no special treatment. But God has combined the members of the body and has given greater honor to the parts that lacked it, so that there should be no division in the body, but that its parts should have equal concern for each other. If one part suffers, every part suffers with it;

if one part is honored, every part rejoices with it.
Now you are the body of Christ, and each one of
you is a part of it.

—1 CORINTHIANS 12:21–27

Conflicts typically begin with a handful of people upset with the church's leadership or direction. Members get angry when they don't fully understand what is going on in their congregation. The key is to keep normal disagreements from escalating to an explosive level where churches disintegrate.

The year Luis and I were married, the mission board we joined thought we would benefit from experience in American church life before we set out to serve the church in Latin America. We were sent to a small congregation in the San Francisco Bay Area. Our assignment was to serve wherever we were needed. After all, we were trained and ready!

The truth is, we were young and naive. Neither of us, especially me, had been involved in a church conflict. On the night of the big congregational meeting, Luis and I were there to "reason together" and deal quickly with the issue. My only outstanding memory forty years later was that it was most unpleasant. The adolescent daughter of the pastor stood on a chair and yelled, "You can't talk about my daddy that way! He loves you people. He prays for you," and stomped out. What a way to begin a vocation in Christian service.

We learned that as individuals, and corporately, Christians are a work in progress and much that shows itself to be the church is in name only. We learned that peacemaking is a gift of the Holy Spirit, and is often in short supply while carnality is upfront and extremely ugly. Motives for leadership can become compromised.

On Sunday morning, many believers ask themselves, "Why should I go to church in light of _____?" (Fill in the blank with whatever conflict is happening at your church.) Though they have not lost their faith, many Christians leave the church convinced they will grow better spiritually by removing themselves from the problems afflicting the corporate body of believers. Alan Jamieson, author of *A Churchless Faith*, termed this trend as "post-congregational" Christians.

The church is filled with people and their accompanying human imperfections, quirks, faults, and insecurities—a breeding ground for conflict. Yet Jesus Christ established the church for our benefit! Completely walking away from the church is akin to throwing the baby out with the bath water.

It's Nothing New

Disputes and divisions were part of the first century church. Jesus, John, Paul, and Peter devoted a large part of the New Testament to instructing Christians how to get along. Hebrews 10:24, 25 exhorts, "And let us consider how we may spur one another on toward love and good deeds. Let us not give up meeting together, as some are in the habit of doing, but let us encourage one another—and all the more as you see the Day approaching."

Lest we be overly shocked by the squabbles, scandals, and debates in local churches, remember that this is not a new phenomenon. Serious issues in the congregations he had nurtured prompted the apostle Paul's letters. Despite the quarrels and public scandal in the Corinthian church, Paul addressed his letter "To the church of God in Corinth, to those sanctified in Christ Jesus and called to be holy, together with all those everywhere who call on the name of our Lord Jesus Christ—their Lord and ours" (1 Corinthians 1:2). The church has always been composed of searching, immature, flawed, but forgiven individuals.

Even in Paul's day, people were prone to drifting away from their regular getting-together time. Imagine that! How contemporary! Solomon said, "There is nothing new under the sun" (Ecclesiastes 1:9). We think we alone in the twenty-first century have urgent issues, have outgrown the need for assembling together, and have a hundred other excuses for why we don't attend church.

We need to take disharmony in the local church seriously because God does. His Son died to make the one Church and all its multiplied congregations possible. Satan and his minions are constantly spreading the news of our disagreements far and wide. Visiting in small towns, I'm amazed to hear how good are people's memories concerning lurid details about who said, or did, what and when in the church community.

Speaking well of the family of God locally is our privilege. It makes people thirsty for what we have found in the church—and that is Jesus as Savior and heaven as our eternal home. Focus on the many positives. Turn negatives over to Jesus Christ and trust him. If you are an elder or deacon, then you must act. But as an individual Christian, follow New Testament guidelines for dealing with concerns and questions while you pray for those in authority.

In our gathering together, we encourage each other, catch ourselves up short from time to time, commit to change, practice spontaneous acts of kindness, and in our connectedness we strive to be more like the one in whose name we meet—the Lord Jesus Christ. There are disciplines that are practiced only in the fellowship of other believers, and there growth takes place best. Uniquely, we profit from meeting together, "For where two or three come together in my name, there am I with them" (Matthew 18:20).

To live above with saints we love,
Why, that will all be glory!
To live below with saints we know,
Now that's another story.

—ANONYMOUS

What Others Say about Church

As long as any of us are breathing, we will offend and be offended. The bottom line is that neglecting the church is folly indeed. The church is a fragile entity, much like a crib mobile with many "arms" that are fluid and susceptible to the slightest movement of air. The local church not only reflects the hope Jesus Christ came and died for, but the paradoxical needs of its pilgrims who are both salt and light, and, at the same time, deeply needy and disarmingly frail.

When the church is experiencing problems, I bathe the situation in prayer. When new leadership changed the constitution of our church, a number of us prayed about it, waited, and eventually met to put it back together based upon Scripture. It was vital that we did not react.

We prayed and bided our time until God opened the door to make changes. During the years of waiting and praying, I focused on the Lord, on Scripture, and on finding the positive in our church body.

Three women in our ladies' group were concerned when the church board sent out a letter stating who could participate in the group and who could not. The new rules left a few women outside the circle. When I approached the pastor and told him a couple of us were concerned about some ladies being left out, he accused us of gossiping. Though we assured him we had not gossiped, one of us was stripped from teaching Sunday school, and the pastor and his family shunned all three of our families. One by one, each of our families left to find a more welcoming church.

The episode sparked an investigation by the elders who found out that many families had been similarly wounded. During a series of meetings, the elders confronted the pastor and he eventually stepped down.

Two books, *Toxic Faith* and *Churches That Wound*, helped me understand that the church body is made up of less than perfect people who sometimes control, enable, victimize, and betray. In other words, the church is made up of people who need a Savior.

The reality of the church is that we find ourselves thrown together with a group of people whom we don't know. Our single common denominator is Jesus Christ. Conflict is our opportunity to put the hard commands of the Bible into practice by submitting to one another, forgiving each other, and considering others to be more important than ourselves. Conflict is the opportunity to practice grace.

Music is one of the most common points of division in the churches I've attended. I've seen people leave a church because the music was too old-fashioned, and I've seen people leave a congregation because the music was too contemporary. There have been controversies over whether instruments like drums had a place in worship, and whether participants could, or should, clap or raise their hands during songs. Some churches tried to do one service with hymns, and a second service for those who prefer contemporary styles.

As a professional musician, I was asked to be the music minister for my church. Immediately people began to lobby for the style of music they considered appropriate for the worship hour. I have done my best to include each one's request, making our music an eclectic blend of hymns and contemporary pieces.

The story is told about a Christian who visited a farmer to talk to him about Jesus Christ. "I won't come to church," the farmer stated. "I know two neighbors who claim to be Christians and they don't live any differently than I do. I'm as good as they are. The church is full of hypocrites."

Months later the Christian went to the farmer to buy a hog. The farmer showed the man all his best hogs. The Christian selected the runt.

"You don't want that one," the farmer protested. "He's the worst runt in the litter."

"I sure do," replied the Christian. "Now what if I take this runty pig from your farm and tell folks this is the kind of hogs you raise?"

"That's not fair!" the farmer exclaimed. "I have some nice hogs. You can't judge my farm by that runt!"

The Christian replied, "If it's fair for the church, it's fair for the hogs!"

Often we judge the church by the hypocrites as if all Christians are like them. When you see only the weaknesses in the lives of your Christian brethren you are doing what Abraham Lincoln described when he said,

"When you look for the bad in people, you will surely find it." Anytime I take my eyes off Jesus Christ and instead focus on people, I will be hurt and disappointed.

In a small fishing village on the North Sea coast of Scotland, a squabble resulted in part of a family attending one church while the other part went to another church. For decades, when these siblings saw one another, they crossed the street to avoid even speaking. After thirty-five years the issues of the conflict had dimmed, but the village had observed the church's uselessness in resolving the problem. No wonder Jesus prayed so fervently the week before his death that we would be one as he and his Father are one, "that all of them may be one, Father, just as you are in me and I am in you. May they also be in us so that the world may believe that you have sent me" (John 17:21, 22).

Living in a very small community, I don't have the option of going to another church. This limitation makes me appreciate the privilege of going to church and spurs me on to help the church work together. Much like a marriage, my church doesn't always meet my needs, but that is not what it is there for. If I focus on the needs of others and serving Jesus Christ, my attitude about church is much improved.

Conflict begins with a handful of upset people. To keep normal disagreements from becoming a firefight, I encourage disgruntled people to take their concerns directly to the person they are unhappy with as Scripture teaches in Matthew 18:15–17. "If your brother sins against you, go and show him his fault, just between the two of you. If he listens to you, you have won your brother over. But if he will not listen, take one or two others along, so that 'every matter may be established by the testimony of two or three witnesses.' If he refuses to listen to them, tell it to the church; and if he refuses to listen even to the church, treat him as you would a pagan or a tax collector." The goal is to clarify the misunderstanding before many people are pulled into a situation. Gossip will die without an audience. Those growing spiritually will have no desire for gossip.

I often wonder how both sides in a church dispute can claim emphatically that they have "the mind of the Lord" and be prepared to go to any lengths to defend their "knowledge." Someone has to be getting and giving the wrong message.

It is difficult to work with people who have differing opinions from my own and conflict can arise quickly. But the Lord invites us to come to him and he will give us rest. Each week I come to church to rest in the Lord and to rest with the other people who have also come into the house of the Lord. Resting together on the pews, we resemble the adjacent stones of God's temple sitting beside one another.

Samuel is my example in times of conflict. Even though the people of Israel habitually turned away from God, Samuel persevered in his job, tenaciously praying for and teaching those who wandered spiritually. Resolving conflict begins with my own spiritual endurance. My job is to pray, encourage others in their spiritual walk, and serve within the church. I must be spiritually disciplined to earn the right to be heard.

The deacons in our church held a series of workshops focusing on issues like anger, alcoholism, chronic illness, and depression. Members of our congregation who had experience in these areas spoke on these topics followed by a question and answer time and then prayer. Suddenly, people in our church began to understand the struggles others faced every day and why they reacted and behaved as they did. This process reduced the amount of conflict occurring within the church.

Having spent years on the mission field, thirsty for the worship and teaching of a church home, I am amazed at the conflicts occurring in the churches back here in the United States. People take for granted the freedom we enjoy to worship corporately.

I have come full circle through a very dangerous journey. The church I attended for several years had two instances of mass casualties under immature, self-serving leadership. The consequences were devastating. Many truly dedicated, mature believers were neutralized and scattered, several taking years to reconnect to the body in a meaningful commitment, including myself. Why is a strong, dedicated follower of Christ so vulnerable to such a whiplash when authorities fail to lead in a godly manner? Are we that fragile that we cannot move through these experiences without a spiritual crack-up?

It has been a very real shock to see firsthand how debilitated many of us found ourselves, how paralyzed and gun-shy and reluctant to jump back into the stream. I am grateful for the wonderful church where I have landed, where I am challenged and loved. I feel safe and have recommitted my life to Jesus Christ. Others of my friends are still trying to find a long-term church home.

I come to church to pray and to worship Jesus and no one can stop me, no matter how mad I may be at things that are not being handled well at the church. I must keep my focus on the eternal majesty of the Lord Jesus Christ, not on the temporal struggles common to every group of people—even the church.

> *Just as each of us has one body with many members, and these members do not all have the same function, so in Christ we who are many form one body, and each member belongs to all the others.*
>
> —ROMANS 12:4, 5

The Church and
Reconciliation

*Whenever I abandon the church for a time, I am the
one who suffers. I grow colder rather than hotter. My
faith fades, and the crusty shell of lovelessness grows
over me again. So my journeys away from church
have always ended back inside.*

—PHILIP YANCEY

As the body of Christ, the church functions at its
finest when it serves as a trauma center for emotional and spiritual emergencies. This may include treatment for broken hearts, calamity-induced concussions,

circumstantial shock, strained relationships, verbal malpractice, and a lacerated sense of self-worth.

Jesus knew his followers would struggle over many things. In his conversation with his Father the night before his crucifixion, Jesus prayed for those future generations that would believe in him. More than once Jesus mentioned the great struggle for unity. "Holy Father, protect them by the power of your name—the name you gave me—so that they may be one as we are one" (John 17:11).

Jesus added: "My prayer is not for them alone. I pray also for those who will believe in me through their message, that all of them may be one, Father, just as you are in me and I am in you. May they also be in us so that the world may believe that you have sent me," (John 17:20, 21). The world is inclined to believe when they see unity in the church.

Jesus knew us well. He prayed for our unity knowing that we would often not put our best selves into the effort. After Simon Peter made the clear declaration of Christ's deity, Jesus promised, "on this rock I will build my church, and the gates of Hades will not overcome it," (Matthew 16:18). The commitment comes from the Lord. He cares about the Church. He gave his life for her, not just for us as individuals but for all of us together throughout all nations and all generations.

It only takes a few seconds to open profound wounds in persons we love, and it can take many years to heal them.

—CHURCH BULLETIN

What Others Say about Church

A young woman accepted Jesus Christ as her Savior during a church service. Though alcohol, drugs, and prostitution colored her background, the change Christ made in her life was quickly evident. As a faithful church member involved in ministry and teaching young children, she eventually caught the heart of the pastor's son. As they began wedding plans, many in the church did not think a woman with her past was suitable for a pastor's son.

A church meeting was called. As the people made their arguments and tensions increased, the young woman's past was paraded in front of everyone and she began to cry. The pastor's son stood to speak. "My fiancée's past is not what is on trial here. What you are questioning is the ability of the blood of Jesus to wash away sin. Today you have put the blood of Jesus on trial. So, does it wash away sin or not?"

Too often we bring up the past as a weapon against our brothers and sisters. Forgiveness is a foundational part of the Gospel of Jesus Christ. That's why it is called the Good News. Second Corinthians 5:17 says, "Therefore, if anyone is in Christ, he is a new creation; the old has gone, the new has come!"

Regarding conflict and sin, our church adhered to a set of standards that the matter was as private as private goes and as public as public goes. Private matters remained private between the church staff and the person involved. If the conflict or sin was public, if it showed up in the newspaper, then it was public before the church congregation.

Emotions escalated and our church became embroiled in a firefight that led to a church split. Though I was asked to leave the elder board, my wife and I stayed in that church. It was hard, but we felt strongly that God wanted us there. It was years before I had tangible evidence that I had acted in obedience. We've not been sorry that we stuck it out.

As a member of our church worship team, I found myself Sunday after Sunday looking out over the congregation and judging the people sitting there. I became too distracted over what was happening in their lives to concentrate on my own worship time with the Lord. One day during my prayer and Bible reading time, the Lord reminded me that he had not called me to judge my fellow believers. He had called me to love them. Changing my attitude towards others helped me to forgive and reconcile with people in my church, many of whom did not even realize that I was judging them.

After our church experienced years without growth, characterized by a revolving door of members coming and leaving again quickly, the church board invited an outside ministry to evaluate the situation. A history of not dealing with problems was brought to the surface and leadership began to deal with conflict in a healthy fashion. It was beneficial to seek outside counsel.

Three principles aided our church in matters of reconciliation. First, people needed to leave church each week saying, "I heard about Christ, not an organization, or a personality." Second, the church was a ministry to the people. Third, church members were committed to one-on-one, face-to-face, life-to-life, people-to-people, and heart-to-heart.

Every church has areas of ministry where they excel. Our church attracted wounded churchgoers and church dropouts, laypeople and leaders who had left their congregations. The church is the only institution that shoots their own wounded—not in the foot, but in the heart.

Our pastor understood that wounded people need a place to come and heal for six months to a year before they are ready to reenter church ministry. These wounded warriors need a compassionate ear to listen to them. They need others to pray with them on their journey toward healing and to challenge them to examine their own role in failure. They need time to process their feelings of anger and betrayal without pressure to serve.

The Bible describes Christians as vessels who are sometimes being filled, sometimes being poured out, and sometimes sitting on the shelf. Grace is the healing balm of Gilead to a wounded soul.

Conflict led to a painful church division and many of our fellow believers left, and for good reason. But God is a master of using all things for good. When the early church suffered persecution and the believers were scattered, God used that circumstance to take the Gospel throughout the world. In the same way, those fellow Christians who left our fellowship are now scattered seed, taking the Gospel abroad and proving that God indeed works tremendous good and blessing through these disappointing experiences.

A member of our church's leadership fell into immorality and, with deep regret, the pastor brought the situation before the congregation. Following repentance, the elders removed this person from leadership yet asked the member to stay within our church. Several years later, after demonstrating spiritual growth, the congregation reinstated this former church leader with a big party. Our church walked out the Gospel's promise of second chances.

Aware of tragic situations that had become news headlines, our church established a policy of doing a background check on anyone who would be teaching a class or supervising children. An ounce of prevention is worth a pound of cure.

Scripture encourages believers to be better church people. Throughout my long life I've seen many conflicts within the body. At this stage in life, I can say remaining faithful to the church, through its ups and downs, was worth it all.

During the tempestuous sixties and seventies, my spouse and I struggled over the desire to maintain my position as church treasurer while dealing with our misbehaving adult children. Our family had been active in this church for many years, so it sparked a controversy when the pastor asked me to step down because my children were not following Jesus Christ. Though we felt devastated, my wife and I resisted the urge to leave the congregation completely. We reared our children in the nurture and admonition of the Lord as best we knew how, but we could not control their behavior as adults. Years later, the pastor has gone on to be with the Lord, our children have returned to the fold, and my wife and I are senior leaders in the fellowship that has remained our church home.

In the midst of conflicts between fellow Christians, we seldom think of the grief God must feel. Observing our own children fighting gives us the smallest taste of how it hurts our heavenly Father when his children squabble. How will we live together in eternity when we hate each other on earth? The source of bitter disagreements is usually sin. Our first line of reconciliation is to pray and repent of our own wrong attitudes including pride and fear of change. In the midst of our God-given diversity of gifts and service, God commands us to live in unity. God gives us grace and love to accomplish the task.

I have been a pastor for over forty years. People often tell me that they no longer attend church because the church failed to meet their needs, often in times of stress such as unemployment. In bitter disappointment, they reject the church. I also see people who appear at the church in times of illness or crisis looking for a particular outcome. They remain as long as the crisis exists. Then they drift off, either because they did not get the answer they wanted, or because they did. When people come to my church asking for help, I tell them, "The church is not here to solve your problems. The church is here to come alongside, to teach you to know Jesus Christ in such a way that you find your own answers."

I have friends I respect highly who view issues differently. We agree to stay off those subjects and love each other. As I grow in my faith, I can become rigid and entrenched or I can love as I draw lines more carefully. To avoid knee-jerk reactions that typically lead to conflicts, the most loving act I do for those in my fellowship who have strong personalities and different opinions is to wait twenty-four hours before commenting or reacting.

During a difficult time in our church, right after our pastor died, Christian "friends" (two couples and a single) were offended by my husband's leadership style. They refused to speak to both of us, complained to the other pastor, and insisted my husband remove himself from all leadership in the church. My husband did as they requested and tried to resolve the conflict with the pastor's help, but to no avail. Friendly and forgiving by nature, I continued to greet them each time I saw them at church only to be met with stares and quick exits. It was excruciatingly painful for my husband and me. The Psalms became our balm.

We were committed to being in church every Sunday, no matter what. Some Sundays it was very difficult to go, and I often quietly wept during the service. But during those years God taught me to enter his sanctuary literally and figuratively, claiming his protection of my thoughts and purifying my worship. He taught us to wait on him and his work, not our own efforts. God never directed us to change churches and neither did they, or should I say we were all too stubborn to leave?

Praise God we all stayed, as over time he changed their hearts and we are friends today. I cherish God's healing and restoration of those relationships.

Angry at a personality trait in my pastor, I left the church. When the pastor met with me to ask what the problem was, months of pent up frustration spewed out while the pastor humbly listened. He apologized, promised to work on improving, and invited me back if I wanted to return. He prayed with me that the Lord would guide us both, then left. It was an emotional time for him as the pastor approached others in the church to ask what additional areas he needed to improve.

Months later, the Lord showed me that I wanted my pastor to have my organizational bents, but God had created him to be people-oriented. The church welcomed me back and reinstated my previous ministry position when I returned a year later. The pastor had considered my concerns, I had matured, and the church kept a bridge between us so I could come back.

It was an important lesson for me to remember that people sometimes make mistakes when they leave a church. We must keep the door open so they can come back. Even if God moves someone out of my church and on to another one there is no reason to behave badly toward him or her.

The watching world is aware of Christian acrimony. Unbelievers often remark, "You Christians can't get along. Look at the number of different denominations you have." Details of debates and discord in our churches quickly spread throughout the community. Dishonorable activities regarding finances and sexual misbehavior are headlines on television magazine features, newspapers, and magazines. I know of two instances where churches divided for less than honorable reasons. After the dust settled, cooler heads prevailed and the congregations rejoined. It was refreshing to have the newspaper send a reporter to write about the amazing reconciliation that united two congregations back into one.

Jesus is my example for how to respond to people who are wounded and hurting. When everyone else shunned lepers, Jesus touched a leprous man. When religious leaders wanted to stone the woman caught in adultery, Jesus tenderly instructed her to sin no more. When people judged the prostitute who washed the feet of Jesus, he said she would be remembered for her service to him. Jesus gave grace.

"Father, forgive them." This may be the most perfect statement spoken at the most perfect time since God invented the gift of language.

— BETH MOORE,
Jesus, The One and Only

Is It Time to Leave?

There are a few valid reasons for leaving a local church:

- *heresy about a pivotal doctrine such as the divinity of Jesus Christ or the authority of Scripture*
- *blatant immorality (whether theft, adultery, or whatever) left undisciplined, unresolved, or ignored* (see 1 Corinthians 5:11)
- *deadness that threatens the spiritual vitality of one's children*
- *starting a new chapter in life and moving to another area*

—LUIS PALAU

While we can remove ourselves from the church, can we remove the church from ourselves? So much of our culture reflects the powerful influence the church has on our lives.

Sunday and church are woven into the fabric of our nation, even though many have abandoned both. People continue to say, "Sunday's coming" and refer to their "Sunday go-to-meeting clothes." How many of us can still show a child the finger rhyme, "Here is the church, here is the steeple. Open the doors and see all the people."

The story is told about a man who was shipwrecked on a deserted island. At last, after years of living alone, a ship arrived to rescue the castaway. As the ship set sail away from the island, the captain asked his passenger, "Are you certain you were alone on the island?"

"Quite certain," the castaway assured.

"Then why are there three huts on the island?" the captain asked.

"Well," the man explained, "the first hut is the one I lived in. The second hut is the church I went to. The third hut is the church I used to go to."

Though we can all smile at the theoretical castaway, are there legitimate reasons to leave the local church?

God calls the church to "aqua-esce" in God's mission—to leave the harbor, lift anchor, and launch out into the joy and risk of the deep sea. Our mission

*is not to hug harbors, or drop anchors where it is
safe, or cheer as other boats sail into the deep. The
place for the church is on the high seas where it is
turbulent and dangerous, where storms gather with
their fiercest intensity.*

— LEONARD SWEET,
A Cup of Coffee at the Soul Cafe

What Others Say about Church

Christians can get caught up in various winds that blow
through the church fanned by the latest spiritual fads.
For several years a segment in our congregation believed
they could solve problems by casting out demons rather
than by confessing sin and repenting. It was easier for a
man to have a demon cast out rather than have to deal
with sins like pornography in a Bible-based manner. I
viewed this preoccupation and overemphasis on spiritual
warfare as rebellion when those involved, like the people in Nehemiah 9:26 and 2 Chronicles 36:15, 16 refused
to listen to those who said, "Go back to the Bible." I
debated the decision to leave the church, but decided to
remain to provide balance for those who were new to
the faith and easily swayed by deviant winds of doctrine
that blow through the church.

Economic realities in our area are challenging, especially for the younger and middle/lower-class families. The financial strain has crushed their dreams and forced them to relocate. They simply can't make it here financially. Our church membership has lost a number of active families due to this and the continuing economic downturn is increasing pressure on others to look at living elsewhere. Like economies, churches have up and down cycles.

"This too shall pass" has become my motto when I am tempted to leave my church. The congregation has wrestled over a multitude of issues from Calvinist versus Armenian views, pre-tribulation rapture versus post-tribulation rapture, and generational sin. Sometimes a concept is true, but believers were not meant to camp and spend the winter there. The truths of God are so amazing and mysterious that we are meant to keep moving on to the next truth we read in Scripture. Christians are individuals in a process who need grace while learning to balance truth with an open mind that realizes that we will not perfectly systemize everything God has said to us. It is not worth the heat and pain to fight about issues not related to the person of Christ and his work on the cross for us.

Like Joshua, who was deceived by the Gibeonites when they told him, "This bread of ours was warm when we packed it at home on the day we left to come to you. But now see how dry and moldy it is" (Joshua 9:12), our pastor was deceived by false teachings that he in turn promoted from the pulpit. Our family decided to remain in the congregation because the youth pastor was an excellent, biblical teacher who was having a positive influence on our children and teenagers. In the process of passing the baton of faith to our children, my spouse and I were concerned about the effect that changing churches would have on our children. Because my children were happy, we opted to calmly and clearly tell the pastor how we saw this issue, and proclaimed our allegiance to this body despite our differences.

Certainly there is a time to leave a church. It is time to leave a church when you are helping to start a new one, to plant, to increase.

A sign posted above the door of our non-denominational church reads, "Come and see." A second sign is posted above the door as the congregation exits that reads, "Go and tell." That church is a sending church. The leadership strives to equip every person sitting in the sanctuary to go out and impact their world for Jesus Christ. Rather than everyone in the church getting behind the pastor's vision, the leadership supports the calling of each church member. As a result, everyone in the Sunday service is involved in some sort of community outreach. When someone from the church will be in a new location due to vacation, mission trip, job relocation, or even prison sentence, the church gathers together and prays corporately, commissioning those going out as missionaries to wherever God has called them.

> *In the pioneer days of the West, we found it an unfailing rule that after a community had existed for a certain length of time, either a church was built or else the community began to go downhill.*
>
> *Nothing else will bring such pure joy and satisfaction, unless it is just pure amusement. Therefore, on Sunday go to church. Yes, I know all the excuses; I know that one can worship the Creator and dedicate oneself to good living in a grove of trees or by a*

running brook or in one's own house just as well as in a church, but I also know that as a matter of cold fact, the average man does not worship or thus dedicate himself. If he stays away from church he does not spend himself in good works or in lofty meditations…. He may not hear a good sermon in church, but unless he is very unfortunate, he will hear a sermon by a good man.

Besides, even if he does not hear a good sermon, the probabilities are that he will listen to and take part in reading some beautiful passages from the Bible, and if he is not familiar with the Bible, he has suffered a loss which he had better make all possible haste to correct. He will meet and nod to or speak to good, quiet neighbors. If he doesn't think about himself too much, he will benefit himself very much, especially as he begins to think chiefly of others.

— THEODORE ROOSEVELT,
from the article "Shall We Do
Away With Church," *Ladies Home Journal,*
Copyright 1917, The Curtis Publishing Co.

There's No Place Like Home

Everything I need to know about the church I learned from Noah's Ark:

One: *Don't miss the boat.*

Two: *Remember that we are all in the same boat.*

Three: *Plan ahead. It wasn't raining when Noah built the Ark.*

Four: *Stay fit. When you're six hundred years old, someone may ask you to do something really big.*

Five: *Don't listen to critics; just get on with the job that needs to be done.*

Six: *Build your future on high ground.*

Seven: *For safety's sake, travel in pairs.*

Eight: *Speed isn't always an advantage. The snails were on board with the cheetahs.*

Nine: *When you're stressed, float for a while.*

Ten: *Remember, amateurs built the Ark; professionals built the Titanic.*

Eleven: *No matter the storm, when you are with God, there's always a rainbow waiting.*

Twelve: *It may stink on the ark, but it sure beats the alternative.*

—CHURCH BULLETIN

It is folly to neglect the local church. On a recent Sunday morning, the idea crossed my mind that because of a hard week, perhaps I would just sleep in. After all, in my line of work, it isn't as if I don't have enough spiritual input.

What you just read is *dead wrong!* Yes, that idea has crossed my mind more than once, but I do not yield. Being part of a church family is one of the few clear mandates of the New Testament. I may be busy about kingdom business all week, but nothing takes the place of, or excuses me from, being part of a local church.

With all the good things to do with our lives, it is easy to consider the church optional. Phantom church members offer many reasons for neglecting the assembling of themselves together: "actually, I go several places" or "I'm in between churches" or "this church doesn't meet my needs" or "we have a different pastor and I liked the old one better."

If someone asked me, "How do you know that the story of Jesus is true, that he is the son of the living God, that the Resurrection is true, and that the Word of God is speaking to us?" there is one simple answer— *the Church!* The fact that the essence of the Good News has been preserved for over two millennia and the light has never gone out on the truth is the strongest and most reassuring foundation for my faith. I am part of a diverse, vibrant, growing family.

Having been in the same church for nearly six decades has given me some perspective. I have learned that:

- given enough time, I get used to changes in worship style and preaching.
- this is my church family and I can't bail out anymore than I can from my biological family.

I come each Sunday to:

- celebrate the resurrection of Jesus Christ.
- set an example to my children and grandchildren.
- be a blessing to others.
- be still and know that he is God.
- worship the Trinity and no awkward program can thwart my access to God.

- be obedient to God by assembling myself together (see Hebrews 10:25) with part of God's family, not some self-designed alternative.
- be known. If my family has a crisis and we need help, the church had better be able to recognize our name.

In our great country, we have a multitude of great resources to make us better and stronger believers, but only one local church. I never give myself a day off because I know my own weakness in making excuses. In all my years, I have heard a lot of great spiritual messages on a myriad of subjects, but I still have a long way to go to arrive at spiritual maturity. Growth is invisible, but real. Obedience is its own reward. I am blessed in my own home church to see long histories of family growth. I love the biblical phrase, "in the fullness of time."

At the end of most Sundays, before bed, a widowed mother gathered her seven children in the main room of their tiny home for prayers. The hymn they sang, sometimes in English and sometimes in Spanish, was an old one:

The day thou gavest Lord is ended,
The darkness falls at thy behest;
To thee our morning hymns ascended,
Thy praise shall sanctify our rest.

We thank thee that thy Church unsleeping,
while earth rolls onward into light,
through all the world her watch is keeping,
and rest not now by day or night.

As o'er each continent and island
the dawn leads on another day,
the voice of prayer is never silent,
nor dies the strain of praise away.

The sun that bids us rest is waking
our brethren 'neath the western sky,
and hour by hour fresh lips are making
the wondrous doings heard on high.

So be it, Lord; Thy throne shall never,
like earth's proud empires, pass away.
Thy kingdom stands, and grows forever,
till all thy creatures own thy sway.

> — "The Day Thou Gavest, Lord is Ended"
> by JOHN ELLERTON (1826–1893)

Far away, at the ends of the earth in Argentina, Luis Palau's family sang a hymn that reminded them of the Church's broad reach and the final words of the Lord Jesus before his ascension, "Therefore go and make disciples of all nations, baptizing them in the name of the Father and of the Son and of the Holy Spirit, and teaching them to obey everything I have commanded you. And surely I am with you always, to the very end of the age" (Matthew 28:19, 20).

What an amazing thought that over all the ages since Jesus Christ's ascension, the light of the Gospel has never gone out. It has been dimmed in places and times as people worship in secret—often paying for that privilege with their very lives. It has burst forth, overcoming great obstacles to grow and thrive in every corner of the world. What God so marvelously nurtures and empowers, we cannot neglect or discount. As Samuel Sebastian Wesley penned, "And someday, the church victorious shall be the church at rest."

There shall always be the Church
And the World
And the Heart of Man
Shivering and fluttering between them,
Choosing and chosen,
Valiant, ignoble, dark, and full of light
Swinging between Hell Gate and Heaven Gate
And the Gates of Hell shall not prevail,
Darkness now, then
Light.

— "The Rock"
by T.S. ELIOT (1888-1965)

Now to him who is able to do immeasurably more than all we ask or imagine, according to his power that is at work within us, to him be glory in the church and in Christ Jesus throughout all generations, for ever and ever! Amen.

—EPHESIANS 3:20, 21

About the Authors

Pat Palau is a winsome and frequent speaker to women's groups, pastors' conferences, and evangelistic luncheons and dinners. In addition to writing and speaking, Pat Palau has partnered with her husband, Luis Palau, in international ministry for four decades. A graduate of Multnomah Bible College in Portland, Oregon, with a BA in Education from Seattle Pacific University, Pat has a heart for evangelism.

Pat and Luis initially traveled to South America as missionary/evangelists with Overseas Crusades (now OC International), then formed the Luis Palau Evangelistic Association in 1978. Crusade invitations have taken their ministry to Latin America, Europe, Asia, Africa, and throughout the United States. Luis has preached to hundreds of millions of people—face to face and via radio and television broadcasts. From the first crusade in late 1966 to the present, nearly a million people have made public commitments of faith to Jesus Christ. The Luis Palau Evangelistic Association's vision is to proclaim the Good News, mobilize the church, and equip the next generation.

Pat and Luis have four grown sons, four daughters-in-law, and nine grandchildren (at last count!). The Palaus make their home in Portland, Oregon, near the international headquarters of the Luis Palau Evangelistic Association.

Pat Palau
Luis Palau Evangelistic Association
P.O. Box 1173, Portland, OR 97207
(503) 614-1500
www.palau.org
lpea@palau.org

PeggySue Wells is a speaker and the author of *Holding Down The Fort*, and *What To Do When You Don't Know What To Say,* both Bethany House publications, and *What To Do When You Don't Know What To Say To Your Own*

Family, and *What To Do When You Don't Want To Go To Church,* both AMG publications. PeggySue was a contributing writer to *Young Believer Case Files* by Tyndale House Publishers. Her articles have appeared in the *Bible Advocate, Church Libraries, The Christian Communicator,* and the *Secret Place.* PeggySue is the author of the *Gaither Pond Video Series Unit Studies.* The homeschooling mother of seven children (known in concert as The WELLSpring Fiddlers), PeggySue writes from her home in Indiana.